Expert Strategies for Serious Hunters

SUCCESSFUL GOOSE HUNTING

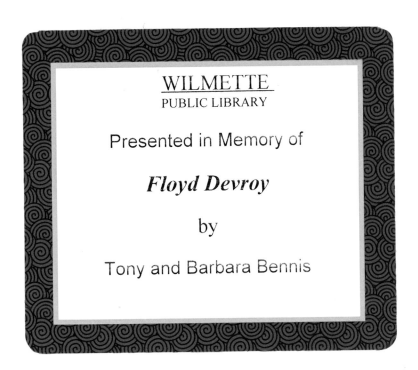

M.D. JOHNSON
Photos by Julia Johnson

©2004 by M.D. Johnson

Published by

An imprint of F+W Publications, Inc.

700 East State Street • Iola, WI 54990-0001
715-445-2214 • 888-457-2873
www.krause.com

Our toll-free number to place an order or obtain
a free catalog is (800) 258-0929.

Library of Congress Catalog Number: 2004093870

ISBN: 0-87349-647-7

Designed by Jon Stein
Edited by Kevin Michalowski

Printed in the United States of America

Dedication

*This book is for everyone who has ever stopped,
mid-step, and turned skyward at the sound; hoping
for just a glimpse, but secure in the sound alone.
You know exactly who you are. And why.*

Introduction

More random thoughts before getting started

Let me ask you this. How do you introduce someone to a sound? Not just any sound, but an *immediately stop what you're doing and find the source* type of sound. A Mother halting in mid-stride because she thought she heard her infant whimper…from three rooms away. A scratching inside the walls just as you're drifting off to sleep AFTER you thought you caught the last mouse in the house kind of sound. It's an attention-grabber, all right. So tell me. How do you introduce a sound like that? Better yet, how do you describe it?

That, folks, was my dilemma and my task here with this, our fourth project, *Successful Goose Hunting*. How to explain what that sound, be it the low-pitched *her-onk!* of the Canada, the two-note yelp of the specklebelly, or the almost mind-numbing barking of 1,000 snows, does to a person? It's like trying to paint a picture with words of, say, Mardi Gras or New Year's Eve in Times Square. What am I saying? You just gotta be there, man. You just gotta be there. There are things in life that you simply HAVE to experience firsthand, and geese are one of them.

Sure, folks will argue that, but they've never been there. How do I know? You just look in the face of a man who's been in the eye of the twisting, turning, swirling tornado that is 5,000 snow geese coming to light on a decoy spread. You look at the face of the guy who's laid next to a shivering black lab dog in a soggy cornfield as a dozen giant Canadas cup their wings and collectively drop those big webbed feet. Look at the eyes of the same man who hears a far-off *honk* on an October morning when the steam rises from his coffee cup as he steps out the backdoor and the maple leaves have taken on the hues of a million painters' palettes. The eyes glaze slightly, and he's overcome with that legendary but all-too-real 1,000-yard stare as he scans the sky. He picks it apart, section by section, just hoping for a glimpse, a brief look at that which made the sound. He doesn't have to say a thing; fact is in some cases, he can't. He knows, and you know he knows. Just by looking at him. He's been there-done that. It's that Goose Hunting Jones, that addiction, and he wouldn't have it any other way.

During the course of this project, Julie and I have had the pleasure of meeting and spending time with some of the best goose hunters in the U.S. and Canada. From hardcore professionals like Illinois' favorite son, Tim Grounds, and famed call-maker and decoy carver…and fellow Ohioan…Fred Zink to hard-working, white collar guys like our good friend, Ben Scott, who just dearly loves everything that goose hunting is about, we had a chance to meet them all. One common denominator that tied all of these, I'll call them Goose Guys, together is that they are nice guys. The kinds of people you'd *want* to spend time with in a pit, a fenceline, or a layout blind. I didn't see the egomaniacal attitudes so often seen today, though talents such as those possessed by Grounds, Kelley Powers, Allan Stanley, Craig McDonald, and a long list of others could certainly lend themselves to such. I saw competition where competition was called for, but a competitive spirit that was infused – not distilled, for the competition on stage was always intense – with camaraderie, advice, suggestion, education, and, when needed, empathy. What I didn't see was the dog-eat-dog, *To hell with the other guy*, on top at ALL costs kind of bullshit – Sorry, but it's my book – that, unfortunately, you do see today whenever and wherever there's any type of competitive event. With almost no exceptions, these guys speak highly of one another, and that's a huge check in the Plus Column for hunters and for the hunting industry.

I think, however, what impressed me the most about the men I call the Goose Guys were the young ones. The Young Guns, I started calling them. Scott Trienen. Richie McKnight. Kelley Powers. Bill Saunders. Ben Holten. Sean Hammock. Talented they are, certainly, but they also possess something you don't see very often, regardless of the industry – professionalism beyond their years. Professionalism, and an eagerness not only to learn, but to share the knowledge that they've acquired with anyone who shows even the slightest flicker of interest. Their passion for the out-of-doors is intoxicating and, fortunately for those who will listen, myself included, contagious.

So that's it. That's the reason behind *Successful Goose Hunting*. It's more than the mechanics – the how-to, when-to, and why-to. Yes, it's about the *Sound*, the call of fall that to many epitomizes everything wild. But it's more than that. It's about the men who follow the Sound. Men who not only listen, but hear it and understand it. Who need it like a side-alley junkie needs another fix. The men who stop, regardless of what they're doing, and turn their faces skyward hoping, some maybe praying, to join sound with sight. This is not only about what they do and how they do it, but why. And therein lies your answers. I only hope that we, with the help of these incredibly talented men, can provide you with some of those answers.

M.D. and Julie Johnson…and friends
October 2003

Table of Contents

Introduction 4

Foreword 6

Acknowledgments .7

Chapter 1 – Meet the players 8

Chapter 2 - Clothes and gear 17

Chapter 3 – Inside the blind bag 31

Chapter 4 – Great goose guns 42

Chapter 5 – Decoys: The art of deception 57

Chapter 6 – The things we remember 77

Chapter 7 – Speaking the language 82

Chapter 8 – Hideouts 94

Chapter 9 – The species and the seasons 108

Chapter 10 – From field to feast 129

Appendix I – 141

Foreword

From Faint Honks To Far Horizons
By Roger Sparks, former editor, Wildfowl Magazine

Like most people on earth, M.D. Johnson is younger than me. When I first hunted with him some years ago on the Platte River in Colorado, I considered M.D. a kid, yet I liked what I saw – a genuine appreciation of the world of waterfowling before and after the trigger pull. I soon learned that this young outdoor writer could put words on paper better than most but, more importantly, he had paid his dues in muddy sloughs and frozen fields. This is another fine book in a series written by a knowledgeable and conscientious author who truly has "been there and done that," and I hope you enjoy it.

In my 50 years of hunting I have not hunted brant, but I've shot the other geese from Manitoba to Mexico, California to Connecticut. Whether I view them through a windshield or down a barrel, the big birds still thrill me – all of them – every time.

As a Midwestern farm boy, I would watch a rare flock of geese pass overhead, first listening to their haunting cries, then finding them high in the blue and following them to the distant horizon. The spellbinding experience scratched my soul, igniting an ancient flame I didn't understand but really liked. Most of those first flocks were springtime snows while a small bunch or two of Canadas might be spotted in the fall. I spent several years with shotgun in hand before I even saw my first speck.

What a contrast between then and now! Snow goose hunting – particularly during once-unheard-of spring seasons – often involves six or more hunters in field setups. The shot is typically called when a couple of Ross' geese drop straight into a string of hunters on the right while several shooters on the left must reach a second line of wavies at marginal range. The decoying is rarely the classic stuff of dreams but, amidst a thousand swirling, screaming white geese, the adrenalin flows, to say the least. Meanwhile, the ubiquitous Canada, with some of its brethren becoming so numerous as to create a serious problem, provides grand decoying in nearly every state. Likewise, white-fronted geese have also prospered, to the great pleasure of hunters from the prairies to the southern wintering grounds. The only questions remaining in all this are the plight of the tundra geese – snows too numerous for their food sources and certain populations of Canadas that are declining for whatever reason. On the whole, though, geese are doing quite well, thank you, and these are, indeed, halcyon years for the North American goose hunter.

In my younger days, I was in awe of the great birds. Listening to the staccato yelps of distant snow goose – among the wildest of all birds – bristled my neck hairs. The yodels of my first flock of specks left me wondering what in the world they could be. As I recall, however, it was a bunch of big Canadas locking up and dropping with incredible control and grace into a neighbor's cornfield that did me in. I knew then, someday, I would become a goose hunter. And I've never been the same since.

Today, there are many pictures of geese in my home; art prints of live birds adorn my walls, and photos – mostly of dead birds – fill most of my albums. Although my wife disagrees, I just don't see how one can have too many goose pictures.

And, a respectable number of birds still make it to my freezer each fall. There are few finer moments in life than a sunrise over stalks or stubble, particularly with goose music in the air. And then they come to the decoys – tilting, talking, always looking for danger. The added pressure we have placed on them has not made them *smarter* as we sometimes say, but they do seem considerably warier than in the past. As they set their wings high above and then circle around behind the spread, the farm-boy hunter in me prays they'll come back around, spill air and slide right in.

But another part of the hunter in me really doesn't mind if they slide off to the side. I think M.D. Johnson knew both sides of a goose hunter long before I did.

I still watch the birds fly over me. When they talk, I feel an ancient urge to call back to them. And whether I am picking the last tomato of the summer or lying in camo in a frozen cornfield, I still look up and marvel at them, always wondering where they have been...and where they are going.

RS

Acknowledgments

More than any of our first three book projects, *Successful Goose Hunting* was a cooperative effort — an accumulation of things seen and heard, learned and forgotten, failed and proved. The experience was lived.

I like that word – accumulation. Maybe it applies to a pile of field-worn decoys shadowed in an off-season corner of the shed. Or perhaps the rag-sleeved canvas coats hanging at the back of the closet. An olive-drab satchel containing a mish-mash of shotshells, benchwarmers from the previous season, or a shelf lined with baseball caps, each aged by time and weather, frustration and triumph. Not a collection, mind you, for a collection is much too orderly, too precise, too inflexible. No, accumulation is the right word.

And it's the right word, I think, to describe the folks who helped foster this project along. The ones who took it from telephone conversation to bookshelf. These are the people who were there when a flag was little more than a black rag on a stick, and the words *short reed* were used to defined a clump of cattails that hadn't grown up yet. These are the innovators. The instigators. And the educators. They're the ones we've admired, and the ones we've disagreed with. Everyday people with extraordinary talents *and* the insight to see how vital it is that they continually pass the torch to the next and the next and the next in line. They're self-started businessmen, minor league ballplayers, farmers, student teachers, and former insurance salesmen – all different, and yet all sharing one very powerful common denominator.

These are the goose hunters. And they're damn good at what they do.

And with that, a heartfelt Thank You –

To Tim Grounds – Thanks for not cleaning my clock when I told you in Kramer, North Dakota, I thought "Those Crazy Ducks" wasn't all that good. Yours are the footsteps in which many have followed, like it or not. I can't say *thanks* enough for your time.

To Randy "The Flagman" Bartz – A true gentleman, and one who understands the importance of the Next Generation.

To Bill Cooksey – I think the strobes would have worked on geese had they been a little bit bigger and a little bit brighter. Keep working on it, Bill. You'll get there.

And thanks for all the doors you've opened and all the help you've been. Oh, and thanks for not being mean, like Allan.

To Fred Zink – Remember the 1,001 questions I said I was going to ask? Well, sir, I haven't even scratched the surface yet. Nice to have a fellow Ohio boy on board.

To Shawn Stahl – If your patience in the goose pit is one-quarter what it's been with me and my myriad questions over the months, then I understand completely why you're as good as you are at what you do. Thanks for all your time.

To Scott Trienen – You exemplify the new breed of goose hunter, young man – the group I kindly refer to as the *Young Guns*. Yours is the future of goose hunting, and we greatly appreciate your time and expertise. Go Scrappers!

To Roger Sparks – Know it or not, sir, I've learned quite a bit from you over the years. Thank you for a wonderful foreword, and all the journalistic opportunities you've afforded me over the years.

To Ben Holten and Chad Eidson – For being both excellent sources of information *and* top-notch photographers, Julie and I thank you for your help and expertise…even if you're making us home-sick on a regular basis!

To Chris Paradise, Rob Paradise, Frank Lovich, Jeff Foiles, Jordan Bowell, Kelley Powers, Hunter Grounds, Kevin Howard, L.P. Brezny, Paul Sullivan, Bill Saunders, Allan Stanley, Richie McKnight, Rod Haydel, John Vaca, Barnie Calef, Christian Curtis, Ron Latschaw, Lee Harstad, George Lynch, Sean Mann, Tony Toye, Paul Thompson, and to all of you not mentioned by name but with whom I've had the sincere pleasure of sharing a blind in the 25 years since I killed my first Canada goose – It's been through your unselfishness, your knowledge, and your passion for waterfowl and waterfowl hunting that I've become, in large part, the person that I am today. **THANK YOU** for everything you've done.

And to Julie. My partner, my wife, my biggest supporter, and my best friend. It's been a long road since Ridgefield, Vantol's, and the Lower River Road, eh? We'll get back soon, you'll see. And then I won't stand up so you can't shoot! I love you.

1
Meet the players

When they close their eyes, *this* is what goose hunters see.

Perhaps I should have spoken of the rule earlier. I would, however, like to preface this statement by saying that this isn't my rule. I'm neither the originator nor the individual solely responsible to see that all people, hunters especially, follow the rule. It would be nice if there were such a person and perhaps somewhere, out there, there is; however, I'm not him.

And what, pray tell, might be the rule? Simple. The proper term is CANADA goose. Not Canadian goose, for we see very few long-necked geese wearing little red coats or drinking Labatt's Blue. Now, it might be correct to say that a Canada goose hatched on a pond outside of Winnipeg, Manitoba, Canada, is a Canadian Canada goose. And while certainly descriptive, the Canadian Canada goose thing is quite wordy. So with that all said, I'll return to my original point – Canada goose is correct; Canadian goose is wrong. However, if you're prone to referring to those brown gamebirds that live in the thickets of northern Wisconsin, Michigan, Vermont, and Maine as *ruffled grouse*, well then by all means – Canadian goose.

With that behind us, we can continue meeting the players.

The Canada goose

I think I'm going to be pretty safe when I say that for the majority of you folks reading this, your first exposure to geese and goose hunting came courtesy of one of the country's subspecies of Canada goose. For many, the Canada defines the word goose. It's the one we're most familiar with, both visually and aurally. Here's the bird that put the *honk* in *honker*, and the one that's earned himself the reputation of the big game animal of the water-fowler's world.

Today, there are 11 recognized subspecies of Canada goose residing in the United States.

All look relatively alike – long black neck, white cheek patch, light chest, dark back and flanks, black legs, black bill; however, there are differences between the races. The most notable of these is size, both height and weight. Color variations can and do exist among the subspecies, but these differences are primarily limited to the chest and flank areas as opposed to an all-over color scheme. Distribution, too, is a variable, and can be helpful when it comes to differentiating between the members of the Canada family, a family which includes from largest to smallest –

Giant Canada (*Branta canadensis maxima*), a.k.a. Honker or Giant – Our largest Canada goose, the Giant was thought to be extinct around the middle of the 20th century; however, members of the population were identified in the 1960s, and have since increased in number as to be problematic in some areas of the central and east-central U.S. The Giant lives up to his name, often weighing between 12 and 18 pounds, though 20-pound specimens, while uncommon, are encountered annually. Like all Canada subspecies, the Giant features the trademark black neck and white cheek patch, along with a grayish chest, medium to dark brown back and flanks, and white underbelly. The legs and bill are black. Again like all of the subspecies, the Giant Canada sports the very distinctive white chevron or 'V' on the rump. Call is the classic low-pitched *honk*, or as it's often described – *HER-RONK*.

Western Canada (*Branta canadensis moffitti*), a.k.a. Western or Westerner – During my time in Washington state (1993-1997), it was the Western Canada that replaced the bird I grew up with in Ohio, the Giant Canada. Myself, I could see little difference between the two visually, the primary factor here being chest color, or in voice; however, Westerns did, as a rule, seem a bit smaller than did my native Giants – eight to 11 pounds versus the Giant's dozen or more. The Western makes its home in the upper West and Pacific Northwest, where it nests and resides in portions of British Columbia, northwestern Alberta, Washington, Oregon, Idaho, western Montana, Wyoming, California, and Nevada. Research shows a large portion of the Pacific population of Western Canadas – the other is known as the Rocky Mountain Population (RMP) – to be non-migratory; however, those that do travel do so between northern breeding grounds and wintering areas as far south as northern California.

Interior Canada (*Branta canadensis interior*), a.k.a. Todd's or Hudson's Bay goose – The most numerous of the Canada subspecies, *canadensis interior* can be found from the eastern edge of the Dakotas damn near to the Atlantic. Other than the Giants I grew up with

West Virginian, John Leep, with a pair of southern Ohio giant Canadas.

in Ohio, this is the Canada I'm most familiar with, as are many goose hunters living in the Mississippi and portions of the Atlantic flyways. He's a relatively large bird, at eight to 11 pounds larger than most, but still shy on the scales compared to the Giant. Lighter by far on the chest than either the Taverner's or the Western, the Interior closely resembles the Lesser in coloration.

Atlantic Canada (*Branta canadensis canadensis*) – True to its name, the Atlantic Canada is, like the greater snow goose, a bird of the Eastern Seaboard. In size and coloration, the Atlantic very closely resembles the more common Interior Canada. From breeding grounds in eastern Quebec and the coasts of Newfoundland and Labrador, the Atlantic travels to traditional wintering habitats in southern Nova Scotia and onto the Pamilico Sound of North Carolina. Concerns for the Atlantic Canada population in the latter part of the 20th century saw seasons closed; however, numbers have increased to where today, limited hunting opportunities are available in Maryland, Delaware, and other locales.

Dusky Canada (*Branta canadensis occidentalis*), a.k.a. Dusky – Even darker breasted than the cackler, often showing no discernable coloration break between the lower neck and upper chest, the dusky Canada is another subspecies limited to Alaska, Canada, and the Pacific Northwest. Specimens will commonly

These birds, photographed in a southwestern Washington field, are either Westerns or Taverners, two of the more common Canada subspecies found in the Pacific Northwest.

weigh between six and eight pounds; however, larger ganders can weigh as much as 10 pounds. Dusky Canadas nest only in the Copper River Delta region of Alaska, with those that do migrate out of the state doing so only as far south as Oregon's Willamette Valley not far from Portland. In 1964, an earthquake in Alaska raised the level of the Copper River Delta, initially creating more favorable nesting habitat for the dusky; however, over time, this change from wet to dry allowed for greater predation on nests and young, as well as adults, by native predators such as bears, foxes, and coyotes. With dusky populations today ranging from 10,000 to 18,000, hunting opportunities, though available in southwest Washington and northwest Oregon, are extremely limited.

Vancouver Canada (*Branta canadensis fulva*) – The Vancouver Canada of British Columbia is particularly interesting as it is, for the most part, non-migratory. One of the larger subspecies, with adult ganders weighing upwards of 12 to 14 pounds, these secretive, coastal forest-nesting geese make their home in southeast Alaska and BC – and there, most of them stay. Those that do migrate do so little farther south than Oregon's Willamette Valley or perhaps the northernmost reaches of California. To tell the truth, little is known about the Vancouver Canada, only that clear-cut logging, and not so much hunting pressure, is one of their biggest and most real threats.

Aleutian Canada (*Branta canadensis leucopareia*) – Another Canada of the Pacific Flyway, the Aleutian is quite similar to the cackler in coloration and to all the Canada subspecies in overall appearance, although in size – up to six pounds – can differ slightly. In many cases, a wider white ring or collar at the base of the neck can help with identification. At one time, Aleutians were listed as endangered under the federal Endangered Species Act, as foxes introduced by fur ranchers onto the birds' home islands off the coasts of Alaska and Asia decimated populations; however, in 1991, their numbers risen from an estimated 800 birds to more than 7,000, Aleutians were removed from the list and given instead, threatened status. Today, few Aleutians stray outside their Alaskan breeding grounds, although some will be seen – but not legally hunted – each year along the western edges of Washington, Oregon, and northern California.

Lesser Canada (*Branta canadensis parvipes*), a.k.a. Lesser – East of the Cascade Range in Washington, goose hunters speak of big geese – Westerns – and little geese, these being the Lessers. Like the Taverner's and Richardson's to follow, Lessers will average six pounds, more or less, and will in voice be higher-pitched than will the larger subspecies. Identical in overall appearance to each of the 11, the Lesser will exhibit lighter chest and underbelly tones than, say, will cacklers, Taverner's, and most certainly, the dusky Canada. The states of Washington, Oregon, and California winter the

An Interior Canada stretches his wings.

majority of the Pacific Flyway's Lesser population; however, birds on the easternmost fringe of the range can be found south to Oklahoma and Texas.

Taverner's Canada (*Branta canadensis taverneri*), a.k.a. Taverner's or Tav – Still another *canadensis* of the Pacific Flway, the Taverner's, or Tav as it's commonly called, is quite similar to the Lesser in appearance, the only differences, however slight, being size – the Tav is somewhat smaller, yet still in the six-pound class – and coloration, the Taverner's being a bit darker breasted than its relative. An Alaskan nester, Taverner's winter primarily in Washington and Oregon west of the Cascades.

Richardson's Canada (*Branta canadensis hutchinsii*), a.k.a. Hutchies – Though here in Iowa, our Canadas are primarily of the Interior variety, we will from time to time encounter flocks of what folks here refer to as "little geese" – the Richardson's Canada, or Hutchie. Noticeably larger than a cackler at five to six pounds, Hutchies show a much lighter (gray) chest and underbelly than do their smaller relatives. The source of some of the confusion may lie in the Richardson's high-pitched *bark*, something altogether different than the larger Canada's well-known and very deep-voiced *honk*. Hutchies are a bird of the Central Flyway, ranging from the High Dakotas south to Oklahoma and coastal Texas.

Cackling Canada (*Branta canadensis minima*), a.k.a. Cackler or Squeaker – Growing up in Ohio, I'd always read that the cackler was about the size of a big drake mallard. It's not that I thought the folks who wrote such things were liars but, having grown up on a diet of Giant Canadas, I never imagined a goose, let alone a Canada, that was "the size of a big drake mallard." But when Maggie brought me my first Washington-state cackler in the Fall of 1994 and dropped it at my feet, my only response to her fine retrieve was – "Maggie! We've killed a baby goose!" I knew I hadn't, but…well, they're just so small. They are small, with most birds weighing from three to five pounds at maturity. Overall, cacklers are all Canada visually, with the exceptions being an extremely short neck and bill in comparison to other subspecies, and a noticeably darker chest (brownish versus gray). Their call, too, is different – a high-pitched sound that I'd say resembles more of a *yelp* than it does a honk. Eastern Washington guide and call-maker, Bill Saunders, refers to the cackler's call as a *cry*, a very accurate description indeed. Cacklers are unique to the Pacific Flyway; specifically, from western Alaska south to the central valley of California.

The white geese

Much press has been given the snow goose in recent years due to a wildly increasing population that is literal-

Similar in size and appearance, several of the *middle* subspecies can be difficult to differentiate. These are probably Interiors.

ly eating itself out of house and home on the slow-to-recover Arctic nesting grounds. This is the lesser snow goose, mind you. Not the greater or the Ross', though Ross' will often be found in the company of lessers. And then there's the blue goose. A separate subspecies? No, but rather a color phase of the lesser snow goose, much as the black squirrel is a color phase of the gray squirrel, and not an entirely different animal. But to explain a bit more in-depth –

Lesser Snow Goose (*Chen hyperborea hyperborean*), a.k.a. snow or white goose – Currently, waterfowl biologists recognize five populations of snow goose: Mid-continent, the greater snow goose (discussed later), West Central Flyway, Western Canadian Arctic, and Wrangel Island. Fowlers in the U.S. encountering lesser snows will in all likelihood be gunning members of the Mid-continent population, of which researchers estimate there to be three million to perhaps six million individuals. Where the Central and Pacific flyways meet, you'll find the West Central birds, while the Wrangel Island – that's off the coast of Siberia, by the way – population winters along the Washington and Oregon coasts, down to northern California. A portion of the Wrangel Island population migrates only as far south as Port Susan Bay, Washington, where hunters enjoy limited yet often very frustrating opportunities during late November and into December.

The all-white lesser snow is aptly named, the only portions of his anatomy *not* colored as such being a pink bill, which features a broad black "grinning patch," pink legs and feet, and black wingtips. In contrast, juvenile snows, often called *gray geese*, will appear as having been held over a smoky fire for some time, as their head, neck, flanks and upper back will be a light gray. Snows aren't a particularly large goose, with most specimens weighing from five to 6.5 pounds, and as such aren't especially difficult to kill; however, their proclivity for flying in huge flocks – 5,000 birds isn't uncommon for one group! – and fondness for wide, open feeding fields often make them a difficult proposition at best. Combine these with the fact that band recoveries from lesser snows have shown the birds living to the ripe old age of 15, 18 or even 20 years or more, and now you're looking at a hunter-wise bird that some will tell you is nothing short of impossible to kill.

To hear a flock of 10,000 lesser snows on a roost pond is to understand fully the definition of the word, cacophony, for it seems every bird, regardless of age or status, feels as though he must contribute to the overall aural chaos. And when leaving the roost, either to feed or to continue on a migration, the only term fitting is DIN. The voice of the lesser snow might best be described as a high-pitched yelp – sometimes two notes – *HAH-hah* – not unlike a white-front yet different, and sometimes three notes – *HAH-hah-Hah*.

Yes, that IS the Pacific Ocean that these geese, most likely Westerns, are wading in. Maybe they just like the view from the beach.

Blue Goose (*Chen caerulescens*), a.k.a. blue or eagle head – I put the blue goose in a category separate from the lesser snow goose simply from a visually descriptive standpoint, for as I mentioned earlier, the blue is but a color phase of the familiar white lesser snow, and not a separate species. That said, the blue differs in color from the snow roughly from mid-neck to the tip of the tail. He's a quite handsome bird, with his pure-white head – hence the handle, (bald) eagle head – in striking contrast to his mottled, grayish-blue chest, underbelly and back. The tail, both above and below, are white or nearly so; the primary and secondary feathers, black edged in an attractive off-white or creamish color. Both bill and legs are pink, and like his cousin, the snow, the blue's bill sports the "grinning patch." Interestingly, blues are found only in the Mid-continent population of lesser snow geese, this being the population that ranges from Saskatchewan and Manitoba south to Texas.

Greater Snow Goose (*Chen hyperborea atlantica*) – As the scientific, or more accurately, its subspecies name implies – *atlantica* – the greater snow goose is a goose of the Eastern Seaboard. From its nesting grounds in the Canadian Arctic and in northern Greenland, the greater snow migrates southward to winter along the East Coast from New Jersey to North Carolina, stopping along the way at traditional points that include the St. Lawrence River near Quebec, and the Delaware and Chesapeake bays. In appearance, there is little to no difference between the greater and lesser snow; however, in the hand, greaters will weigh slightly heavier – up to 7.5 pounds as compared to their lighter, six-pound cousins.

And again like their lesser brethren, greater snow goose populations, perhaps due to a moratorium on hunting for several years, have increased to alarming and habitat-endangering proportions. From less than 50,000 in the mid-1960s, the continental population of greater snows has grown to an estimated 800,000 (1999) individuals, and it's feared that this ever-increasing population may have irreversible effects on vital feeding grounds such as salt marsh environments along the Atlantic Coast. Understandably, as numbers have increased, so too have hunting opportunities, both in Canada and in the United States.

Ross' Goose (*Chen rossi* or *Anser rossi*) – The Ross' is the smallest of our white geese, tipping the scales at three pounds, more or less. In size, this snow goose in miniature will equal that of a large drake mallard; that is, turn a cackler snow-white except for the black wingtips and the pinkish bill, and you'll have yourself a Ross' goose. Aside from the size difference, Ross' can be told apart from their larger white relatives by their lack of a black "grinning patch" on either side of their bill. Mature Ross' geese, too, will often show wart-like bumps on their

A small flock of snows passes the blind. Will they swing, or continue heading north?

bill near the base; odd-looking, for certain, and there for reasons perhaps known only to the birds themselves. Ross' are often found in the company of lesser snow geese, though the smaller birds can often be seen in Ross-only groups within larger mixed flocks. While the occasional Ross' will venture east of the Mississippi, the birds are most common in the Central (primary) and Pacific (secondary) flyways.

White-fronted geese *(Anser albifrons albifrons)*

As of this writing, I've killed but two white-fronted geese in the 25 years since I shot my first Canada. The first in 1997 in North Dakota while hunting with Fred Zink, and the second a year later during a freakish three-day windstorm in western Iowa where every duck and goose in the Central Flyway was blown at least 500 miles eastward off-course – but that's another story altogether. My problem with white-fronts has simply been my not being in the right place at the right time. I never saw one while in Ohio, and saw but one during the five years I lived in Washington. Here in Iowa, I'll encounter no more than a pair throughout the whole of the hunting season and get shots at neither; however, during early March, thousands of the boisterous birds will over-fly eastern Iowa on their way to breeding grounds in Alaska, the Yukon, and the Northwest Territories. Frustrating birds, certainly, for someone living in the eastern Midwest; however, they're

one of the most fascinating geese available to hunters in the U.S.

White-fronted geese, also known as white-fronts, specklebellies, or simply, specks, are a strikingly handsome bird. On mature specimens, the black chest barring from which the specklebelly draws its name shows up quite well against the light gray chest and white underbelly; juvenile birds, on the other hand, will show little or no barring. The orangish-pink bill ends in a distinctive white face patch, which in turn gives way to a gray head and neck. A darker gray highlighted with white edgings marks the back and flanks. White-fronts sport yellow or yellowish-orange legs – the only North American goose to do so. Adult white-fronts will weigh five to six pounds, give or take; young birds, slightly less. Two subspecies of white-fronted goose are recognized in the U.S. – the aforementioned greater, seen in both the Central and Pacific flyways, and the slightly larger and darker Tule white-fronted goose *(Anser albifrons gambelli)*, which winters almost exclusively in California.

While specks can occasionally be seen in the central Midwest, they're much more likely to be encountered from the Missouri River west to California. Washington and northern Oregon hunters see few white-fronts; however, to gunners in southern Oregon's Klamath Valley and California's famed Sacramento Valley, specklebellies are a very common part of the bag. Central Nebraska's Platte River and the Cheyenne Bottoms in Kansas are well-

Part of a large flock of snows and blues on a typical South Dakota roost pond.

Strikingly handsome birds, the white-fronted goose certainly does come by its nickname – *specklebelly* – legitimately.

Waterfowling fanatic, Tommy Akin, with an Arkansas speck. Southern folk are absolutely in love with this wonderful bar-breasted bird.

known speck haunts, as are parts of coastal Texas, Louisiana and southern Arkansas.

Unlike Canadas, white-fronts don't *honk*. Instead, their call is a high-pitched, two-note – *HAH-hah*, with the emphasis on the front half, and a slight drop in volume and pitch on the second. Phonetically, it's difficult to reproduce; however, the cry of the specklebelly is akin to the cackle of a rooster pheasant or the bark of a fox squirrel. Once you've heard it, there's no mistaking it for anything else.

2

Clothes and gear

The onset of colder weather can mean improved hunting conditions, but it also dictates a change in the way we dress for the field.

I'm not exactly sure what I was wearing the evening I killed my first goose. I'd say nothing, simply for the shock value, but that's really a visual no one needs. But let's just say that clothes didn't really make the man.

The more I thought about it – what I was wearing in 1979 when I shot my first Canada – the more curious I became about the specifics. So I went back to an old photo album, back to the Polaroid picture that my Old Man shot when he came out to my Babi and Dzedo's – Slovak grandparents – to see this first goose. What I discovered was interesting to say the least, particularly in this day and age of high-tech camouflage. The pants were camouflage, or at least they could be loosely defined as such, what with their mix-and-match blotches of brown, brown, and brown. My shirt was, as best I could tell, a combination of purple and white stripes – a sort of Southwest pattern which, looking back, was probably a bit out of place in a northeastern Ohio cornfield in October. An old canvas coat, complete with the requisite cigarette pocket over left breast, rounded out the ensemble. Where that came from I don't have the slightest idea, but there it was. Oh, and a chocolate brown toque; a watch cap or toboggan hat for those folks who have never seen the movie *Strange Brew* featuring that Canadian duo of psuedo-brothers, Bob and Doug McKensie. Overall, the outfit was as far removed from what the modern goose hunter wears as Bill Gates is from a Seattle soup kitchen. Truth is it looked as though Stevie Wonder and Salvador Dali dressed me before I hit the field.

But that was then, and as folks say, this is now. Oh, there's still those guys who head into the goose field looking like they'd covered themselves with Super Glue and rolled through the bargain bin at the neighborhood Goodwill Store; however, today, these guys are in the minority. No, today's goose hunter – myself included – can

Early season goose hunting typically means short-sleeved shirts and light pants. And bug spray. LOTS of bug spray.

typically be found garbed head to toe in the latest camouflage patterns and technologically advanced synthetic materials. Things with names like Gore-Tex, polypropylene, Thinsulate, and a long list of odd and mysterious monikers, the words along capable of making us wonder if we really should be putting this next to our skin. And dare we get into the ultra-realistic camouflage patterns, combinations of colors and images so incredibly true-to-nature that hunters have actually misplaced body parts while adorned as such – only to find them again when they stood up. What about boots? Gloves? Hats? Long-johns? Do Spongebob Squarepants boxer shorts have a place in the goose blind?

It all brings up an excellent question – What should today's goose hunter know about clothing, camouflage, accessories, and the fine art of, well, getting dressed? Better yet, what's this individual need in order to (1) be comfortable, and (2) be successful? Fortunately, there are answers.

A sharp-dressed man

For purposes of our clothing discussion here, I'm going to separate goose hunting and dress into two elemental categories – warm-weather situations, and cold-weather situations. Certainly there may well be some overlap, such as those high blue-sky October mornings where it's 32 degrees when you're setting decoys and 52

when you're tearing down; still, and for the most part, we're looking at two scenarios – warm, and cold.

Warm-weather geese

This subdivision I'm referring to as *warm-weather geese* is in reality somewhat difficult to define and address in terms of where, when, and how. That is, with cold weather goose hunting, it's a relatively simple matter to advise someone simply to put on clothes until they're no longer cold. If you get too warm, you merely take some off. Easy enough. However, under warm weather conditions and in most parts of the country – and I know damn well this applies in the conservative Midwest – you're running quite the risk if you offer up this advice – Take it off until you're cool....or naked. I can see it now – *Iowa goose hunter jailed for public indecency; thousands traumatized.* Needless to say, it wouldn't be pretty.

So, that behind us, just what would constitute warm-weather goose hunting? Across much of the country, those states that offer early September nuisance or population management Canada goose seasons could be said to be offering warm-weather opportunities. A simpler definition of a warm-weather hunt might be any hunt where geese, sweat, AND mosquitoes occur simultaneously. But travel south of the Mason-Dixon Line, and it's very possible to take part in regular season hunts where the temperatures climb into the 60s and above. And I think most of us would say such outings would fall into the warm-weather category.

That all said, the best advice I can give you in terms of clothing and warm-weather goose hunting is this – Dress light, but throw some *just-in-case* items into your blind bag. By dressing light, I'm talking about light twill britches and a similarly light Henley-style long-sleeved shirt. Why long sleeves if it's hot? Well, chances are it's not going to be hot a half before the half hour before legal shooting time. If that's the case, you'll be thankful for those long sleeves. When it does warm up, just roll 'em up. As for headgear, we'll address that shortly; however, I'd suggest a mesh, sometimes called a summer weight, long-billed baseball cap. The cloth caps, though stylish, can be awful warm during those early September hunts.

Lately, I've taken to wearing what's known in the trades as a *Bug Suit* for most of my warm-weather goose hunting. These innovative articles of clothing – mine comes from the Iowa-based Bug-Out Outdoorwear – are made from a finely woven mesh cloth, and are designed, as the name implies, to provide a barrier between you and the mosquitoes, gnats, chiggers, and ticks that would eat you. The pros to such suit are many. They're lightweight and take up very little space in a blind bag or day pack. Because they're mesh, any breeze circulates through the suit, thus keeping the wearer surprisingly cool. And finally, due to their tight weave, the suits, which typically come in packs consisting of a zippered jacket with a hood and pants, can be worn over little more than a grey t-shirt and still fill all the camouflage requirements any goose hunter would want or need. Hell, I've watched Brad Harris of Lohman Game Calls wear his suit overtop a white – WHITE! – t-shirt during turkey season and never have a single problem getting gobblers to waltz up to the gun. If that's not a testimonial to the effectiveness of the suit, I don't know what is. And, yes. The suits are available in any of several different camouflage patterns.

But back to those *just-in-case* items. These are those things that you'll be glad you have, just in case the temperature goes down, the temperature goes up, it rains…things like that. And so I don't reveal too much of what's contained in the next chapter, *Inside the Blind Bag*, let me stay focused here on articles of clothing that might be a good idea to have along, such as –

A **wool toboggan** or **watch cap** – You never know when a passing front will bring falling temperatures.

A **cheap pair of brown jersey gloves** – See above, plus jerseys make for great inexpensive camouflage.

A **camouflage hanky** or **neckerchief** – Just great things to have for any of 1,001 different reasons.

Sunglasses – If these aren't self-explanatory, you've been in the sun TOO long.

The day had dawned cloudy and cool, hence the reason behind the rain gear and wool pants in September. But early season can mean rapid weather changes – Be Prepared.

Extra pair of socks – Take it from someone who's taken athlete's foot to a whole new level, fresh socks can be a godsend, especially under warm and sweaty conditions.

Are all these items necessary? Probably not, but then again, there's really no reason *not* to carry them with you. They're lightweight. They don't take up a lot of space in your already crowded blind bag. And finally, they definitely fall into the category of "it's better to have them and not need them, then it is to need them and NOT have them." In many parts of the country, warm weather is often fickle weather, and there's no excuse for not being prepared.

Cold-weather geese

The problem, as I see it, with cold weather goose hunting and proper dress is this – You have to wear enough so as not to freeze to death while you're huddled, unmoving, in the blind, BUT not so much that you sweat yourself into a lather while you're setting out decoys…after which, you're afforded the opportunity to watch your perspiration condense into ice crystals and drop off, along with portions of your anatomy. With that in mind, then, how do you dress to stay warm when it's 25 degrees AND stay cool when it's 25 degrees?

A good hunting jacket can spell the difference between comfortable and miserable. Here, Christian Curtis dresses for late September Canadas...in Canada.

Layering. Yes, I realize that it's not a novel concept, but it does work. In the case of cold-weather goose hunting, I'll not only layer, but will actually under-dress initially. That is, I'll wear what I deem sufficient to keep me warm enough while setting blinds, decoys, and what-have-you, but not so warm that the physical activity causes me to – well – sweat up or dampen those garments in direct contact with my skin. But, you're gearing up to say, that ensemble probably isn't enough to keep me warm once the work's done and I've crawled into my hole, is it? And you'd be right, so that's why, once the decoys are arranged, rearranged, and re-rearranged, the blinds set, and everything put in order, I'll add those outer garments that I brought with me *but* as of yet hadn't worn.

So, with that all said, what's M.D.'s cold-weather layering list look like? Well, let's assume that the mercury's running about 25 points; that is, 25 degrees Fahrenheit. Under these conditions, I'll be wearing in order of assembly –

Socks, polypropylene – As you'll see, I prefer thermals; however, synthetics such as polypropylene that work by wicking perspiration away from the body do have their place. And for me, that place is Feet, Layer One.

Carhartt thermal long underwear, bottoms – Even with the advancements in synthetic materials, I remain a big fan of the old-fashioned thermal-style underwear, and Carhartt makes some of the best and most rugged I've found. Too, Carhartt's wide elastic ankle bands help keep

Layer One – socks – from falling into my boots.

Socks, wool – Inexpensive ($4/pair) military issue wool socks are next, and that's usually all my feet want or need. In theory, the poly-pro socks pull moisture, aka sweat, away from my skin where it's trapped in Layer Two, the wool. And everyone knows that the greatest thing about wool is that it retains warmth, *even when wet*. This combo works for me, and works well.

Polypropylene, top – I know what I just said, but I didn't say that I never wear synthetics. This very light, short-sleeved top not only helps keep me warm, but it pulls the inevitable sweat away from my skin during set-up and tear-down.

Carhartt thermal, top, long-sleeve – This goes over the polypropylene top for extra warmth

Union suit – If it's exceptionally cold, and it often is in December throughout much of the country, I'll pull a cotton Union Suit – yes, complete with button-down back flap – overtop the first layers. This serves to somewhat mold everything in place, including the second pair of socks

Sweater, wool – A couple years back, I took to wearing a full-wool sweater from the folks at C.C. Filson as my outer-most cold-weather layer; that is, over the Union Suit and underneath my jacket or coat. Yes, such sweaters are a bit spendy ($189/XL). And, yes, they do require special care, although I've C-A-R-E-F-U-L-L-Y washed mine at home versus dry-cleaning, and haven't had a bit of trouble. Still, if you want something that will last *and* keep you incredibly warm without having to put on 162 inches of clothing, well then I'd suggest a good wool sweater.

Pants, canvas – Paul Taylor in Ohio makes some cotton canvas britches that would appear to have been made with the cold-weather hunter in mind. Designed originally for tree-trimmers and tree climbers, aka arborers, Paul's *Arborwear* pants are as tough as they come, and roomy enough to be worn over several layers of long underwear. Unfortunately, they're not available in camouflage – yet – but do come in greens and browns that would work just fine. No Arborwear? Any rugged pant would do the trick – Carhartt being the first to come to mind – just as long as they'll fit over everything you're trying to tuck underneath them.

Insulated bibs – Here's one of the items I'll add after the work's done and I've crawling in the pit. For the last couple years, I've been wearing Mossy Oak's *Whistling Wings* series insulated bibs, and can't say a bad thing about them except for the fact that in some cases, they're flat TOO warm. Still, they do what they're supposed to do, and that's keep me both warm – insulated – and dry, thanks to a waterproof nylon shell. That said, a couple things about bibs before you buy regardless of manufacturer – (1) Make sure the bibs have good quality clips and studs on the suspenders and chest piece. Nothing irritates a man more than having to quick-fix his suspenders in the dark before a hunt. (2) Trust me on this – You want the bibs with the zippers up the outside of the legs. You stopped fighting your pants over your boots when you were 12, remember? And (3) Get them big enough to fit over the clothes you expect them to fit over, but not so big that you're swimming in them.

Jacket or coat – Used to be, the hunting coat – or rather, the warmth factor of the coat you wore into the field – depended on one thing, the temperature. Elementally, if it was cold, you wore a heavy coat. Not so cold, a light coat. And that worked just fine, except, that is, for that fact that temperature fluctuations required you to have more than one coat. Today, that's all changed. In these modern times, any number of manufacturers – Columbia, Mossy Oak, Whitewater Outdoors, Cabela's, Bass Pro, Browning, and the list goes on and on – no longer offer goose hunters mere coats, but rather what's known in the industry as *Systems*. Systems are actually little more than coats inside of coats and given a fancy-sounding name; however, there are differences between these garments and the outerwear we used to wear. Currently, I'm wearing what's called a **4-in-1 Parka**. Made by the folks at Browning and worn by none other than Phil "The Duck Commander" Robertson himself, the 4-in-1 consists of a rugged, waterproof outer shell made of, among other synthetics, GORE-TEX, along with a reversible – camouflage to brown and back – goose down zip-out liner. Pockets? Plenty, and then some. Spendy? Well, depending on the manufacturer, these waterfowl systems can range from $100 to $300. But before you blow a financial artery, think of it this way. If the weather's mild, you wear only the camouflaged outer shell. If the weather's mild AND rainy, again, you wear the outer shell. Should it be sunny but chilly *and* you're hunting an improvised fenceline blind, the camo inner coat – Remember, it zips out – gets the nod. Downright cold and blowing snow? Well, that's where the entire system comes into play. So in truth and for an on-average cost of right around $175, you're getting four coats capable of handling several different weather conditions, and all for a pretty reasonable price. Now, and with that said, will your old Carhartt insulated coat work? Probably, and in all likelihood, just fine; however, you might want to give these Systems – Hell, call 'em coats…I do – a try.

Let me take just a minute and talk about goose hunting and raingear. For years, and even while living under the perpetual grey skies of western Washington, I never wore rain gear. I simply dressed warmly and got wet. Eventually, though, I realized that getting wet no longer had to be an integral part of the waterfowling experience. Okay, so I'm a slow learner, but I do learn.

And what I learned was that raingear is, in this day and age, a wonderful thing. Gone are the archaic olive-

This young guide along Colorado's Front Range opts for a pair of rag-wool gloves, a good choice even if the weather's damp.

drab and Woodland pattern rain ponchos. You know, the same things that made hunting in the rain damn near like trying to shoot your way out of a big Hefty bag. And relics, too, are the raincoats that, while keeping you somewhat better than flat-out wet – Soggy? – were either incredibly hot or incredibly cold, and as such, pretty much gave you a choice between uncomfortable situations.

Enter – GORE-TEX. Old hat to waterfowlers today, this still-revolutionary material is not only waterproof, but actually helps keep you warm or cool, depending, of course, on the weather. In most cases, GORE-TEX is used as an inner lining; that is, a tough outer shell is mated to a protective layer of GORE-TEX, and it's the combination of the two that keeps you dry, cool, warm, or whatever.

With the introduction of the aforementioned waterfowl *Systems*, stand-alone raingear for the goose hunter has become almost a redundancy; however, I can see situations – early season geese with cool mornings or the hunter living in south Louisiana might be two – where traditional, though modern raingear could certainly come in handy. Too, and in case you're needing to justify the $50-$150 price tag such gear carries, there's no reason these stand-alone rainsuits can't be worn on other occasions – spring turkeys, October squirrels, or your nephew's high school football game to name but three. The bottom line? Get yourself some good raingear. Your non-wrinkled, dry skin will thank you.

Mild conditions like those enjoyed by John Taranto on a hunt near Winnipeg, Manitoba, can call for nothing more than your regulation ball hat.

Head, hands and feet

Name three things that habitually ruin, or at the very least cut short, cold-weather hunts, and I'll be willing to bet that two of the three will be cold hands and cold feet. You'd think in this modern age, what with synthetic fabrics designed not only to wick perspiration away from your body but convert it to steaming chicken-and-rice soup, the days of getting cold in the goose blind were over. Alas, my friends, that's not always the case. What *is* the case in these instances of temperature-related discomfort is improper dress. Plain and simple. And so to that end, I'll address those three topics known simply as head, hands, and feet.

Headgear - Admit it. When you were little, your Mom always made you wear your warmest toboggan hat whenever you went outside to play in the snow. Why? Well, Mom knew that the vast majority of your little body's heat that was lost was done so through the top of your head, and that a good, warm cap would drastically reduce this loss, thus keeping her child safe and toasty. She also knew that it was a complete waste of her time – and yours – to try to explain this from a scientific standpoint, so she simply used her maternal status to convince us that yes, wearing a warm hat on a cold day was indeed a good idea. Not to mention being a lot gentler on the butt than a wooden spoon.

Childhood memories aside, the scientific fact does remain – Most of the body heat that's lost is lost through the top of the head. Wear a warm hat, and this loss is minimized. Conversely, when the weather's warm and heat loss through your noggin is what you need, then a lightweight cover, something that allows the body heat to dissipate, is in order. With that biology lesson still ringing in your ears, here are the hats I wear, along with some approximate temperature readings that I use for guidance. More or less.

Baseball cap, mesh – 50 degrees and up. The mesh back allows heat to escape, and this helps keep me cool during warm-weather hunts. The long bill shades my eyes and hides a portion of my face…which should be camouflaged (see Mister Invisible below).

Baseball cap, full cotton canvas or oilcloth – 35/40 to 50 degrees. Here, the full cover helps hold heat inside on those chilly hunts, but doesn't overdo it.

Watch cap, cotton or blend – 25 to 35/40 degrees. Ah, my old brown toboggan hat, aka The Ultimate Duck Beanie. Fits tight to my scalp like a skullcap so it doesn't interfere with my vision or my shooting, and holds in the heat better than R-50 insulation. Too, and if it's especially nippy, I can pull the hat down over my ears and keep them warm as well.

Bombardier's cap, wool – Very cold to 25 degrees. This is the same hat worn by Phil Robertson, and is about as warm a thing as you can put on your head, short of your Aunt Ethel's cat. What makes these bombardier caps are the flaps, which can be pulled down over the ears and

Don't be misled by the strenuous activity and the accompanying body heat – It's still cold out there! Wind chills in Iowa on this hunt ranged from -18 to really/really cold.

secured under the chin, thus keeping everything nice and warm. My only complaint? With my bomber cap all buttoned down, I don't shoot worth a damn. I can't see. So I simply wear mine up, ala The Duck Commander, perhaps defeating its main purpose; however, I address that fact. Read on.

While we're on the topic of headgear, let me say two final words – neck gaiter. When it's cold enough to warrant either a watch cap or bomber-style headgear, you can bet your last chemical hand-warmer that I've got a gaiter around my neck. Honestly, I don't know how or why I didn't hit on these things earlier because they're absolutely awesome under cold-weather conditions. They're lightweight, come in all the popular camouflage patterns, and keep you warm like no tomorrow. Right now, I'm wearing a fleece wrap from Avery Outdoors. This particular gaiter can be cinched tight against the North Wind, and is contoured so as to be worn high in the back and lower in the front should the wearer wish. A Phil Robertson hat and a neck gaiter? All I can say is bring it on, Mother Nature. Bring it on.

Hands – To tell you the truth, I've never been much on wearing gloves while I hunt. Sitting on a deer stand? Yes, then I'm all for them, but in terms of wing-shooting and wearing full gloves…well, I just never got used to it, I guess.

Still, there are those times when I want for something covering my paws. And during such times, I'll fall back on

but one style – fingerless wool. Whether they're the grayish ragwool or inexpensive military glove liners, it doesn't seem to matter. In fact and on any given day afield, there's a really good chance you can find a pair of each on my person. Why wool? As I mentioned before, wool's warm when it's dry and it's warm when it's wet. Why fingerless? While I'm sure to mention it again, I simply like the feel of my skin – bare skin – against the safety, the trigger, a shotshell, my call….any number of things. Yes, it's probably more mental than anything else, but I also see it as a safety factor. That, and I've always done it that way.

But there's no need to despair, those of you who are looking for a camouflaged glove that will not only keep your hands warm, but has complete fingertips as well. A quick walk through Mack's Prairie Wings, Cabela's, or Bass Pro, and your head will reel with the number of makes and models available today. A couple words of advice, though. One, it's probably best to buy your hunting gloves in person; that is, where you can physically try them on before you buy. When it comes to shooting, proper fitting gloves are damn near as important as is a properly fit stock. And secondly, be sure and give the gloves a trial run BEFORE your first hunting trip. In other words, throw them in your range bag and take them with you the next time you go to the club to shoot a round of trap, skeet, or sporting clays. Better to work out the bugs there than as you're sitting up to shoot as your buddy hollers – Take 'Em!

This old pair of Northlake boots, now tattered and torn, was excellent from mid-season through 'til the end of the coldest January hunt.

A couple final words about your hands. The first is neoprene. Myself, I've never liked neoprene gloves. Regardless of whether they're designed to keep my hands dry while setting decoys or warm and dry under wet-weather conditions, I just simply haven't found a pair that allows me the sense of touch I feel I need to either shoot safely or accomplish tasks of manual dexterity *without* seeming like my fingers have been zip-tied together. Maybe it's just me; however, I did want to mention neoprene as an option.

And finally, hand-warmers. Today, chemical hand-warmers – the little white bags you expose to the open air and shake a bit – have for all intents and purposes replaced the old-style silver-cased liquid fuel models that our fathers and their fathers used and lit their Camels from. Sure we still have the old ones, but it's just so much more convenient to pull, shake, heat, and throw away. Such, I believe, is technological advancement. Nostalgia aside, I would highly recommend setting in a supply of these great little gadgets because they are just that – great. Whether HeatMax, Mister Heater, Heat Factory, or some off-the-wall generic brand, it just doesn't matter. They all work the same, they're cheap, and they'll be the best four bits to a buck you'll spend on cold-weather gear this fall. Simply tuck one in the back of each of your gloves and another in your breast pocket, and you're set. Better than that, slide one of the four-by-five inch models into a fleece hand-warmer, aka hand-muff, and you'll be wondering why you brought gloves in the first place. From someone who's been cold a lot, warm hands make all the different in the world, partner. Trust me.

Footwear – I'll go out on a limb here and say that goose hunters are relatively low on the list of folks who think – and I mean really think – about what they're tying onto the end of their legs before a hunt. No, not everyone's guilty of this, but I know personally that my upland boots, even my on-stand deer boots, get a lot more attention than do my goose shoes.

And it makes sense, doesn't it? Like the infantry grunt, the pheasant hunter earns his keep on his feet. So, too, the western big game guide, the deer driver, and the bunny chaser. Even the duck hunter, clad as he is in his neoprene girdle, lives in his boots to a much greater measure than does the goose guy. Does this, then, mean that the goose hunter shouldn't care about what he's putting on his feet? Certainly not.

Here, I'm going to go back to my warm-weather/cold-weather scenario. For the warm-weather hunter gunning over dry ground, I feel pretty safe when I say that any good quality uninsulated hunting boot will perform more than adequately. Remember here, as with any piece of equipment or gear, that you're going to get exactly what you pay for in terms of quality. That said, I'd take it a step further and recommend one of the recognized brands, names like Rocky, LaCrosse, Redwing, Danner, and the like. What I call mud boots, too, are another option, particularly if your ground or the season comes complete with rain and mud. These calf-high boots are made of rubber, neoprene, or any of a number of synthetics, and are available in camouflage, no-camo, insulated, and uninsulated models. Northerner (Servus) makes a good mudder, as does LaCrosse, Hodgman, and the folks at the Connecticut-based Muck Boot Company. Let me note here before you ask – No, two pair of boots, a hunting boot and a mud boot, aren't necessary, as a quality hunting boot should serve you well, day in and day out, through any kind of weather conditions; still, it's all about options, eh?

In cold-weather situations, footwear may or may not change. I say that because again, a good hunting boot – Rocky's *Cornstalker Pro*, for instance, a model I've worn for some time – should be able to keep you cool in the early season AND warm when the temperatures fall. Instead of buying several pairs of boots, I'd suggest purchasing several different pairs of socks of various materials, thicknesses, and insulating qualities. Good socks, and here I'm speaking of wool, wool blends, and synthetics such as Polypropylene, are what make a quality hunting boot versatile, and are what allow you to go from September through January with warm feet and without putting a hurt on your billfold. The only exceptions to this *Change Socks, Not Boots* mantra that I've found come into play under a couple different conditions. The first is phys-

The same waders you're using for your duck work can certainly pull double-duty for any water-based goose hunting you're going to do

ical; that is, perhaps and for whatever reasons – age, metabolism, health – you have poor circulation and simply cannot keep your extremities, namely your feet, warm. The second has to do with Old Mother Nature. If you're hunting under conditions where *warm* is defined as zero degrees Fahrenheit…well, that would certainly qualify. Here, I'd advise looking into a specific cold-weather boot such as Rocky's *Snowstalker*. For several seasons, I've worn the *Snowstalkers* under some of the most brutal of Midwestern conditions, including a late muzzleloader deer season with straight temps of -10 and wind chills down to -40, and have never once complained of cold feet. Complain? Yes. Cold feet? No. Granted, a pair of *Snowstalkers* will run you from $175 to $200 – NOTE: There are less expensive extreme temperature boots available, and I'd suggest doing your homework before you buy….But you knew that – but, (1) they should last for many, many seasons, and (2) what price warm toes?

A couple final words on boots. First, electric socks. My advice here is simple – Save your money and spend what you save on quality non-electric socks. Maybe things are different today, but my past experience with electric socks has been less than stellar. Typically, they'd work like the devil when you first fire them up; however, they'd more often than not work too well and make your feet sweat tremendously. Then, when your feet were nice and damp, the two D-cell batteries would abruptly die, thus leaving your feet wet and, ultimately, very cold. Here

again, save your money and get good socks. And finally, chemical foot warmers. Like electric socks, I haven't had much luck with chemical foot warmers. At least not when I've used them as directed; that is, in my boots. In your pockets where oxygen can get to them, they work wonderfully; however, in my boots, they quickly fade, immediately thereafter balling up under my instep, making it feel as though I'm walking on beanbags. I'll pass.

I'd probably be remiss here if I didn't briefly mention waders and their place in the goose hunter's equipment inventory; however, I won't spend too much time on the subject simply because, and while I might be wrong – I don't think I am – I believe there are few goose hunters out there who are purchasing waders specifically for goose hunting. Yes, there are plenty of wader-owning duck hunters who cross over into the goose realm throughout the course of the season, and as such, I believe this is where you see your wader-wearing goose hunters. So, and with that said, let me proceed in a couple different directions at this point –

Direction One – You already have waders, probably chest waders, which you purchased due to your interest in duck hunting. If that is indeed true, then those same waders will work just fine should you decide to take your goose show onto the water. How so? Well, maybe you're hunting a small Midwestern marsh for Interior Canadas. Or the Platte River in Colorado for westerns. Or the Lower Columbia for Taverner's. Regardless of the location, if it

That's what I like to see! Your basic, old-fashioned Woodland *blob* camo pattern. And you know what? It works.

can be safely waded, your duck waders will fit the bill just fine.

Direction Two – Let's just say for the sake of argument that (1) you don't already own waders, and (2) you *are* buying waders specifically for goose hunting. Not a problem. Today, chest waders are available from any of several different manufacturers, as well as the major catalog outlets such as Cabela's, Bass Pro Shops, and Mack's Prairie Wings. As you might expect, prices vary depending on factors such as brand, materials, thickness, and camouflage patterns, to name but a few, and will range from $90 on the low end to around $250 for some of the more elite models.

For those of you buying waders, I offer the following suggestions.

Go with chest waders – Yes, they'll be a bit more expense than hip boots, but at least with chest-highs, you don't have to worry about going in over your hip boots. Now, if you're going in over your chest highs, you need to seriously re-evaluate your wading practices…preferably on dry land.

Go neoprene – It's rugged, warm, and won't crack or rot like the old rubber waders. Plus, today's variety, or your choices, are going to come in neoprene. As for the thickness of the neoprene itself – 3 millimeter (3mm) and 5 millimeter (5mm) are the most common – you'll just have to decide how badly you're going to abuse them, and how cold it's going to get where you do the majority of your

hunting. Me? I'm tough on waders *and* a lot of my wading's done in cold water, so I go with the thicker 5mm set.

Go camo – I really don't have to say anything here, seeing as I'm speaking to certifiable camo junkies; still, I'd be the fool if I didn't mention that chest waders come in a variety of camouflage patterns, one of which is sure to appeal to you. 'Nough said.

Go boot foot – Some guys like stocking foot neoprene chest highs; some guys don't. I don't. I like having my boot permanently attached to my wader. Why? It's one less thing I have to worry about forgetting, losing, or any of a hundred other bad things. And a couple words specifically on chest wader boots. One, I prefer a serious deep-cut lug or tread on my soles, as it sure makes the going in muddy, slimy, or slippery conditions a hell of a lot easier. And secondly, insulation. Most of today's boot-foot chest highs come with some type of insulating material, usually Thinsulate. And that's good; however, I'm not sure it's necessary. An uninsulated boot will be cooler during warm-weather hunts, and socks – quality socks – can always make up the difference when the temperatures fall. Your choice, and your wallet.

Go with reinforced knees – Sure, it may cost a little more, but the extra $20 you spend on chest highs with reinforced knees certainly beats the C-note you'll be shelling out the first time you kneel on or run into something bad. Can you say "Barbed Wire in the Dark?"

Go suspenders – Or the shoulder straps that use the

hook-and-loop fasteners. I'm torn here. Suspenders are traditional and usually work well, but they often stretch, need adjusting, fall down, whatever. The hook-and-loop style suspenders are quick to adjust and I've never had them fall down; however, if you wear your chest highs as half or waist-highs, which we often do, the permanently affixed hook-and-loop suspenders are always getting in the way, dragging in the water, and catching on stuff. Too, these styles often have a tendency to rub against your neck, especially when your waders are cinched up high or you have several layers of clothes on. The bottom line? Both do the job, which is holding your plastic pants up, so you decide.

The bells and whistles – I call them bells and whistles almost in jest, as every set of chest waders I own – and that's several – have these features, and purposely so. The first is a chest pocket or pouch that opens side-to-side, NOT from the top. The top-flap pockets are all right for storing things that aren't a serious loss when they fall in the water. This does not include your truck keys, believe me. However, it's awful hard to wrap your cold hands around a hand-warmer AND get them inside a top-flap pocket. With that in mind, go with the side openings. And finally, a belt. Most modern neoprene waders, if not all, feature belt loops through which a nylon webbing belt can be threaded and quick-clipped on your belly. I'm going to make this simple – Get a belt. Wear the belt. The first time you fall, and you will, and the belt prevents your chest waders from filling completely and dragging you to the bottom of the swamp, river, lake, or whatever, you'll be loving that $6 belt.

Mister Invisible – Camouflage

Now don't get me wrong. I like camouflage clothing as much or more than the next guy. Hell, I like the whole aspect of camouflage regardless of how it's worn or what it's on. But think about it for a minute. That is, think about camouflage from a goose hunter's standpoint. You're in a totally enclosed layout or pit blind, itself concealed so as to be damn near if not invisible. What do you need camouflage clothing for? I mean, couldn't you be wearing a clown suit and propeller beanie, and be just as hidden as if you were clothed in the latest and greatest 3-D photographic patterns? For heaven's sake, man, you're in an enclosed hole in the ground, for crying out loud!

Are we little more than slaves to camouflage fashion? To some extent, I would imagine that's true; however, camouflage ourselves as goose hunters we must. In some cases – gunning from impromptu or portable blinds where the blind itself doesn't provide 100 percent concealment, for instance – head-to-toe personal camouflage can indeed be beneficial, and I believe can make a differ-

Goose hunting brother, Tony Miller, becomes as one with a trash bag spread set for snows in northern Washington, proving camouflage doesn't have to be trendy to work well.

ence in a gunner's success or lack thereof. For the most part, however, it's my thought that camouflage as it relates to the goose hunter, when you get right down to it, actually serves two primary purposes. First, there's tradition, or as my old algebra teacher, Mr. Gene Zorn, explained – If A = B and B = C, then A = C. That is, goose hunters (A) are waterfowlers (B). And waterfowlers (B) wear camouflage (C); therefore, goose hunters (A) wear camouflage (C). Thanks, Mister Zorn. If you think about it, it makes sense.

And secondly, and perhaps more significantly, it's my belief that camouflage is as much a psychological factor in the goose hunter's – any hunter for that matter – success or failure as is anything else. Why? Simple. If a man believes himself hidden and hidden well, thanks to whatever camouflage pattern or accessories he might place on his person, that's one less thing he has to think about in the field. He KNOWS he's invisible, and as such, can concentrate on his calling, his shooting, his blind – any of 101 variables other than his personal camouflage. It's all about confidence. If you have confidence in your equipment, that equipment will work at its best for you.

That all said, do I wear camouflage while goose hunting? Yes. Again – why? Well, there is the tradition and the equation above. Plus, there's the outcast factor. After all, I don't want to be the only gunner of five lying in a Canadian pea field wearing blue jeans and a red "I'm with stupid" t-shirt. And, true to my word, I do believe in the

Binoculars have 1,001 uses to the goose hunter. Spy on your neighbor, keep an eye on your truck, see where your lab went, or simply pass the time.

confidence that camouflage gives me. But what do other folks think?

"Even with the new enclosed layout blinds," says Bill Cooksey, head public relations man for Avery Outdoors, "you're going to find yourself in situations….well, how many times have you been caught outside your blind? You're picking up birds, somebody says GET DOWN!, and you find yourself hiding behind the blind. These are the kinds of things that can and do occur in hunting situations, and here, camouflage is still an important thing."

He continues. "In a perfect scenario, camouflage probably isn't an issue unless you're flagging or otherwise exposing some part of your body. There will always be times in the heat of a hunt where parts of you are going to be exposed, and I like knowing that these parts are covered properly." In other words, Cooksey, as well as countless tens of thousands of hardcore goose hunters around the country, aren't much in favor of exposing themselves to geese. And I'll leave it at that…

But back to my personal camouflage. Layout or pit blind or no, I'll still dress in head-to-toe camo. The pattern? That's a matter of personal preference. Let's just say, as the trout anglers do, it's important that you *match the hatch*; that is, try to match your camouflage as closely as you can to the type of habitat or cover you're hunting. Maybe that's Mossy Oak's new Shadow Grass in a Saskatchewan stubble field. Or Realtree's Advantage Wetlands at the edge of a November cattail marsh. Or

Natural Gear's…you see where I'm going with this. Do you as a goose hunter need all of today's camouflage patterns to be successful? No, but because (1) there's a good chance you already have them, and (2) you understand well what I mean by matching the hatch, there's no need to explain.

One point that I will explain, or at least touch on, here is the oh-so-important connection between camouflage and your face. Think of it this way. Take 25 white paper plates and paint one side to match exactly the color of your lawn. Lay them white side DOWN on the grass. Now, climb on your roof so you can see each of the plates, or at least where each of the green plates should be. Wait! A wind comes along and flips over six of the plates, and then just as quickly flips them back over. Despite the fact they were turned for but a fraction of a second, that flash of white instantly caught your eye. It drew 100 percent your attention. Where there was once *nothing*, now there's *something*. And I'm here to tell you, geese aren't attracted to this kind of *something*. My point is this – The flashing white plates? That's what your uncamouflaged face looks like to a goose every time you point your mug skyward "just to look around" or see where the birds went. What you've created is a strobe light, a blinking beacon that shouts – Stay Away From Here!

Remedy? Camouflage. Myself, I'm prone to camouflage make-ups or paints, simply because I don't care to wing-shoot while wearing a head-net. For some gunners,

Being properly outfitted makes it easy to spend as much time as necessary – and comfortably so – in the blind. Far as I know, no one's ever killed a Canada from their living room.

it doesn't matter. Regardless of what style – paint or fabric – you choose, choose one, put it in your blind bag, and use it. Yes, a long-billed baseball style cap can certainly help shade your face to some extent. In fact, and I think I'd be safe in saying in perhaps 75 percent of the situations, you can watch as hunters in layout blinds pull their hats down onto the bridge of their nose as the birds are spotted, believing, as I do, that it's possible to hide a 6-foot, 3-inch, 200-pound body under 15 square inches of hat! Sometimes it works; most times, it doesn't. What does work is when this same hat is used in conjunction with a head-net or with face paint, the result being 100 percent coverage for the 75 percent of those who simply can't keep their heads down. And admit it – that's 100 percent of us…some of the time.

A final point about camouflage, and that's your hands. During the course of a hunt, there are going to be times – calling and flagging are the two that come first to mind – when your hands are going to be exposed; that is, out from under the cover of a blind, a pit, or what-have-you. And just as your face acts as the aforementioned *Keep Out!* Light, so, too, do your white hands, each one flickering and flashing against the darkness that is the interior of the pit or the darkness of the blind. Fortunately, and again, the solution is simple – gloves. Or rather, camouflage of some kind. Personally, and I know I'm not alone here, but I don't like painting greasy camouflage make-ups on my hands and then painting it all over my shotgun, my

calls, the dog, or anything else for that matter. Instead, I'm a fan of gloves. Brown jersey gloves like the kind you get at the local filling station for 99 cents with the fingertips removed. Why the fingertips? Maybe it's purely psychological, but I like the feeling of my bare skin against both the safety *and* the trigger of my shotgun. I just feel more…well, safe, that way. And the El-cheapo 99-cent jerseys? They provide everything I need in the way of camouflage and, when combined with one of the popular chemical hand-warmers, supply more than ample warmth even on the coldest days. And let's not forget the fact that at 99 cents, I'm not too upset when – not IF, but when – I leave them behind in the field at the end of the day. Trust me, it's going to happen.

Field accessories

My dilemma at this point lies in not stealing the thunder from nor giving away too much of the content of the next chapter, *Inside the Blind Bag*; therefore, I'm not going to spend a lot of time here on field accessories. As you'll see shortly, goose hunters – myself included – more often than not pack quite a bit of gear into the field. Each has its purpose, whether it's a compact tool kit capable of performing emergency shotgun repairs in the field, or a Ziplock bag filled with 25-cent oatmeal pies, sunflower seeds, and old Pop-tarts.

That said, I do want to highlight some of items you'll

read about in this next chapter, as well as some of the gear that I personally wear or carry into the field. Of particular note are the items relating to safety or on-site maintenance or repair. Calls, shotshell selection, and the choice between frosted blueberry or unfrosted strawberry Pop-tarts…well, I'll leave that up to you.

Blind bag – This is what everything goes in. More on that in the next chapter.

Neoprene shell belt – I used to think these resembled Pancho Villa's bandoleers and made me look like an FNG. That's *friendly new guy* to all but you Vietnam vets who know better. I've since changed my thinking, and have decided that these belts really are a convenience. Plus at $13 to $14, they're pretty inexpensive convenience.

Ankle gaiters – If you're tried of pulling on your chest highs and having your pants ride up to your crotch, then you need a set of ankle gaiters. For what they do, they're ridiculously cheap and, believe it or not, they're better than duct tape. At least here.

Binoculars – When the birds aren't flying, I like to look around. Compact binoculars bring everything within eyeshot – the next guy's decoy spread, my truck, Jet – who's decided to hunt on her own – not to mention letting me get a close look at distant birds. And yes, those are cormorants…now quit calling.

Gerber multi-tool – This one's self-explanatory, or should be. What's that? You always carry one and have yet to use it? Well, partner, just leave it at home and see what happens. They're good for a million things, and then some.

Emergency kit – In a small (6 inches x 3 inches x 2 inches) flat Tupperware container, I have the following: bandages, Q-tips, safety pins, string, a 24-inch length of rawhide, chapstick, tweezers, a spare truck key, flat-pack of camo duct tape, two emery boards, a flat tin of aspirin, a couple small Ziplock bags, and a squeeze tube of gun oil. Other items may come and go, but these are the essentials and are always in the box.

Before I go any farther, let me stop there in terms of the accessories. As you'll see in the next chapter, these are but the tip of the proverbial iceberg when it comes to taking stock of what this country's goose hunters carry with them into the field. Oh, they're good enough, but they're just the beginning.

All right, one more. Toilet paper. 'Nough said.

Inside the blind bag

The blind bag. Mysterious catch-all for the 1.58 million things that a goose hunter needs.

Blind bag: n. Any of the large satchels carried afield by goose hunters. It is thought to contain all of their worldly possessions. Often cloaked in secrecy, mud, feathers, and dog hair.

Years of evolution, convenience stores, microwave ovens, and Pizza Hut delivery haven't changed the fact that we humans are hunter-gatherers. Yes, sir, just like our ancestors, but maybe with a little twist. The hunter part? That's relatively self-explanatory, perhaps even based on the fact that you're reading and presumably interested in a book on the subject of hunting. But what about the gathering portion of the equation? Well, folks, that's changed just a bit during the

That's Washington's Bill Saunders, here proving that he's as deadly on the white ones as he is on those with stocking necks.

65,000 years since we crawled from the mud and ran about hairy, naked, and stinking of our last meal. And no, I'm not talking about deer camp or three of the four years you spent in college.

I'm talking about gathering. Today, we hunters do a hell of a lot less gathering of food items as did our ancestors – the nuts and berries, roots and tubers that were the staples of their meager diets. Instead, we gather STUFF. And let's face it, we goose hunters are guilty of this stuff-gathering right along with everyone else in the clan. Oh, yes. Gone are the days when pass-shooters went afield armed only with a shotgun and a box of bullets. And as for those who would hunker in a blind at the upwind edge of a decoy spread? Their pile of stuff – all necessary, mind you – would make the strong-shouldered bulls that pull the ox cart look for someplace to hide.

But aside from the obvious, that being firearm and ammunition, and with decoys for the most part a given, just what does all this so-called *stuff* that today's goose hunter is hauling into the field consist of? And what's more, how does he carry it into the field in an organized – Organized? – manner A backpack? A wheelbarrow? Or maybe 18 small children, each assigned part of the pile?

Enter – the blind bag. The blind bag, for those of you who read our turkey hunting book, isn't all that different from the turkey hunter's vest in that both allow you to carry damn near ridiculous amounts of gear into the field, all in one nicely and neatly contained, though at times

extraordinarily heavy, package. The most interesting thing about the blind bag, and again like the turkey vest, is the same as is the case with a soldier's footlocker or a lady's purse – The more you get to digging around in there, the more, well, *interesting* stuff you're going to find in there. Each item, it's assumed, has its purpose. And while it might not come into play today, tomorrow, or the next day, there's going to come the day when Item X is going to be needed…and these guys damn well will have it!

With that all said, I thought it would be interesting – There's that word again – to take a look inside the blind bags of some of the nation's most recognized goose hunters, as well as those of several Man on the Street waterfowlers, a group among whom I proudly count myself. So let's take a look into the depths of these bags of mystery, and see what might be pulled out were you to reach in. And based on what some of these guys carry, I wouldn't be surprised to see a rabbit. Or worse.

Bill Saunders, 2002 Washington State and 2002 Pacific Flyway goose calling champion, and crafter of fine duck and goose calls

- NatGear Final Approach blind bag
- 2 boxes Kent Fasteel 1⅛ ounce BBs
- 1 box Hevi-Shot #4s - I think they were a tip
- Briley Light Modified choke tube for Super X2
- choke tube wrench

- spray can Breakfree gun lube
- Leatherman multi-tool
- staple gun & two boxes of ⅜" staples for pit lids
- black fleece neck gaiter
- pair leather work gloves – I try not to use those
- Two bags of SPITZ sunflower seeds
- Bottle of aspirin
- Cell phone
- Bill Saunders Traffic goose call
- Bill Saunders Reload goose call
- Two Bill Saunders Gravity Duck calls – All on two Hensley lanyards
- Traffic goose call back up in Ziplock
- Speck/ross goose call in Ziplock bag
- Bill Saunders G.P. in Ziplock
- Small bag with backup reeds
- 200 feet of decoy cord with snap for jerk string rig
- Small Mag-Lite flashlight
- Washington hunting regs with shooting times
- Four replacement pins for Final Approach Eliminators
- Roll of toilet paper
- A few sunflower seed shells, rocks, feathers, and a dead beetle, too.

TIP – As of this writing (August 2003), I haven't had the pleasure of meeting Bill Saunders. Hopefully by the time this piece goes to print, that will have changed; however, what I can say even without having formally met the man is that Saunders' personality is one of readiness. Rather, his blind bag contents describe him as an individual who much rather have something and not need it than need something and not have it. As a Type A Personality, I'm okay with that. As for Saunders' list, aspirin. Just one of those small plastic disposable bottles of aspirin, and let me tell you, the contents can literally salvage a hunt.

Jordan Bowell – **Washington goose guide and partner in Aero Outdoors, makers of fine goose hunting products**

- Staple gun and staples - to staple camo to pit lids.
- Zip ties - to hold camo to blinds.
- Garden spray bottle - Pits dry out faster than rest of field, so we spray pits with water to blend. Spray decoys with water to remove frost.
- T-flag
- 3-inch Hevi-shot #2 and/or 3-inch Kent Faststeel BBs
- Gloves
- Fleece hat
- Band-aids

DePalma's inclusion of a face mask, certainly meant as camouflage, might have prevented the author's icy build-up.

- Coke and assorted candies or candy bar.
- Skyjacker short reed goose call, Knight & Hale tube call, custom
- Primos duck call
- Leatherman mulit-tool
- Gun oil
- Energizer LED headlight
- Cookies from my wife

TIP – I found Jordan's mention of a plastic spray bottle filled with water intriguing. I'd never given it any thought at all, but it makes sense that with air circulation from both above *and* below, the lids of pit blinds would dry out and discolor faster than the rest of the field. Think of it this way. Take your shoes and throw them out on the sidewalk. Now, hose the sidewalk down. When you retrieve your shoes, aren't the two places where they were lying – the dry spots – going to stand out like a Styrofoam cup in a coal bin? Likewise, I would imagine, with pit lids. Good call, Jordan.

John DePalma – **Public relations director for C.C. Filson, Inc.**

- Winchester High Velocity 3-inch #2 shot
- Primos Wench duck call - two of them.

Fellow Ohioan and Avery R-n-D man, Fred Zink, suggests carrying a small camera, even a one-time-use model, in the bag as a means of recording the hunt.

- Duck Commander widgeon/sprig call
- Haydel's goose call
- Cabela's leather duck strap
- Face mask
- Innotek collar
- Training bumper – If the dog's muddier than heck at the end of the day, this way I can send him on a retrieve and wash him off
- Energy bar and water
- Small thermos of tea
- Walker game ears
- Gargoyles eye protection
- Game shears
- Leatherman multi-tool
- Fillet knife

TIP – How many times have you been in a goose blind, ratchet-jawing with your partners, when all of a sudden one clams up and hisses – "QUIET! Did you hear that? With the Walker Game Ear, which we've used with great success in the spring turkey woods, you're now able to not only hear the geese at a distance, but differentiate geese from the barking farm dog down the way. Yes, high winds, amplified by the unit and rushing by your ears, can prove troublesome when you're trying to hear; still, on those still or semi-still days, you'll be amazed at what you can hear. Too, the Game Ears serve double duty as hearing protection,

something we as shooters should all be concerned with.

Fred Zink – **World goose-calling champion and Avery Outdoors Pro-Staff Team member**

- Mag-Lite head lamp
- #4 Hevi-Shot for ducks; #2 Hevi-Shot for geese
- Avery neoprene decoy gloves
- Avery fleece neck gaiter
- Mossy Oak Dry-Lite rain suit
- Olympus E-10 camera
- Cell phone in case of emergency
- Spare truck key
- Avery neoprene thermos bottle filled with hot chocolate

TIP – As photography is a huge part of our business, we seldom go anywhere without a camera. Unfortunately, the same can't be said for many hunters, not a few of whom wish afterwards that they'd had a camera to capture the various aspects that made such-and-such hunt a great outing. Today, there's really no reason *not* to carry a small 35mm camera into the field. Quality point-and-shoot cameras like the Nikon N65 with a 28-80mm auto-focus lens – That's the model I use for all my film needs –

will run you $200 to $275, depending on where you shop. Freddie's E-10, a digital camera, will set you back eight to nine bills. Quite a bit of money, yes, but it is digital. On the opposite end of the spectrum, there are plenty of fixed lens point-and-shoots out there for less than $100, and in most cases, these will work just fine for your hunting photography needs. Still not convinced? Well for $5 to $7, you can always pick up a one-time disposable camera. Just shoot 'em up, take the whole thing to the processor, and in a couple days – Voila! Pictures of your hunt. If you're going to go that route, which is an excellent way to go if you're looking to save some green, I would suggest buying a brand name disposable – a Fuji or Kodak or something of that nature.

David Corum – Founder of The Duck Hunter's Refuge at www.duckhunter.net

- Echo Cocobola Timber Call
- Echo Poly Open Water Call
- Victoria Honker Flute Goose Call
- Duck Commander Mallard Drake Call
- Haydel's Wood Duck Call
- 2 boxes each of #2 & #4 HeviShot, 3-inch
- 1 box of Estate Shells BB, 3-inch
- Avery Neoprene Decoy Gloves
- Cotton Jersey Gloves
- Face Mask
- Face Net (Cooler Temps)
- Activated Hand Warmers
- Binoculars
- Mini Mag-Lite Flashlight
- Butane Lighter
- First Aid Kit
- Matches
- Whistle
- Bottled Water
- Snacks (Beef Jerky, Crackers, Cookies)

TIP – Binoculars. Now here's something I don't see folks pull out of their blind bags often, and I can't understand why. A compact pair of armored field glasses weigh next to nothing – eight to nine ounces is about par for the course – and take up very little room in the bag itself. Add the fact that compacts are available in prices ranging from $25 to $225, and everywhere in between, and I'll bet even more of you will be scratching your head and asking yourself, "Why didn't I think of that?" Truth is, you probably have a pair already. If so, great; if not, get a pair. You can always use them for spring turkeys or treestand whitetails; that is, when you're not spying on geese with them.

Lightweight and taking up little space, an extra pair of gloves thrown in the bag can save the hunt...not to mention your hands.

Christian Curtis – Champion goose caller; Avery Outdoors and Rich-n-Tone Pro-Staffer; goose book cover model

- Shotgun shells: Remington Hevi-Shot 12ga. 3 inch #4's
- Lanyard: Coyote Leather
- Goose Calls: RNT Kelley Powers Short Reed Acrylic x 2
- Electronic dog collar: Tri-Tronics / Flyway Special
- Neck gaiter: Avery
- Hand-warmer: Avery
- Gloves: Colombia / Gore tex
- Facemask
- Flashlight: Mag-Lite
- Leatherman All-Purpose Tool
- Thermos: Avery
- Can of Gun Lube: Rem Oil
- Dog Vest: Avery

TIP – I know, I know. It's just a piece of fleece worn around your neck and cinched with an elastic cord and one of those little springy-things used to adjust the length of your decoy lines, BUT – under extreme weather conditions, a neck gaiter is one of the warmest pieces of gear you'll ever put on your body.

Hailing from Sikeston, Missouri, Christian Curtis exemplifies today's enthusiastic and conscientious *Young Gun* goose hunter.

Our first gaiters, designed in the field and born out of necessity, consisted of nothing more than an old wool military surplus scarf cut into 18-inch lengths, with the lengths then pulled over our heads and worn around our necks. We still use the originals today, though I will admit that I'm awful fond of the fleece gaiters from Avery. Regardless, the rule's simple – Get one. Wear one. You'll like it.

Brian Lull – Sales and marketing for the Seattle-based Outdoor Empire Publishing, Inc.

- MTM Shot Shell Dry Box
- Field gun-cleaning kit – choke wrench, cleaning rod, WD40, and small bottle of Rem Oil
- Improved cylinder and modified choke tubes
- Facemask and wool gloves
- Disposable camera
- 1 box of Remington Nitro Steel 3-inch #BBB or #Ts
- Ear plugs
- Nikon compact binoculars
- Motorola Talkabout FRS Radio
- Haydel's DR 85 duck call
- No goose call – That's what I've hired the guide to do
- Sunglasses
- Bottle of water and bag of trail mix for snacking

TIP – What can I say about the "no goose call" quote? The guy's honest. But on the subject of cleaning kits. This is one of those things that you might never need, but if the need arises, you're damn sure glad you've got one. Brian's kit is small, self-contained, and doesn't take up much room in the bag; however, along with his list, I'd include a small set of punches, a couple playing card-sized rags, and a miniature set of needle-nosed pliers. Don't want to put together your own kit but think it's a good idea nonetheless? Down-sized kits such as Cabela's *Tactical Cleaning System* ($35) are available, compact, and work well – I have two from a time before they were Cabela's; however, for $15 or so, you can assemble your own package AND tailor it to your needs specifically.

Ben Holten – Owner, North Flight Waterfowl, a Washington-based guide service

- 2002-03 Washington State small game laws
- Tripod for cameras
- Carmex and Chap Stick
- Canon Power Shot A20 digital camera
- 8 AA batteries
- (2) boxes Kent Fasteel 3-inch 1 ¼-ounce BB
- Bausch & Lomb 12x25 binoculars
- 6 feet of small rope
- Toilet paper
- 2 small pocket knives
- Leather game carrier
- Staple gun and staples
- 2 cans of christmas tree snow flocking
- 20 game transport slips
- Gun lube and gun cleaning rod
- Business cards
- Spare Tim Grounds Half-Breed
- Spare decoy trailer key

TIP – Now here's a no-brainer. Sooner or later, you *are* going to lose your keys in the field. Hopefully they won't be in your pocket at the time they're lost; nonetheless, they will become misplaced. For less than $5, you can get not only Ben's spare decoy trailer key – if, that is, you own a decoy trailer and need a key…Ben's NOT going to give you one for his, sorry – but while you're at the hardware store, have the lady behind the counter make you a spare truck key as well. I think Mister Zink mentioned this earlier. Put both spare keys in one of those little rubber clamshell change purses that old guys carry, and put the thing in your blind bag. I don't even have to say that at some point in the future, you'll be glad you did.

Owner of the Washington-based North Flight Waterfowl, Ben Holten kneels here with a big Canada and his partner, Chad Eidson's, white-front. Nice speck, Chad!

Barnie Calef – Three-time world champion duck caller and Hunter's Specialties Pro-Staffer

- Camo Compact make-up kit – 3-color Hunter's Specialties
- Hot Hands hand warmers
- Waterproof Matches
- Weather Radio
- Gun Wipes – Birchwood Casey Sheath Take-Along
- H.S. Waterfowl choke tubes
- Short Reed Slammer Goose Call
- Custom Short Reed Goose Call
- Snow and Speck call
- Leather Quad Lanyards
- DRYLOK High Velocity Steel 3 $\frac{1}{2}$-inch, 1 $\frac{1}{4}$-ounce
- Supreme High Velocity Steel 3-inch 1 $\frac{1}{4}$ -ounce
- Pocket Binoculars (Swarovski 10x25)
- Folding knife (Gerber Gator-Mate 6252)
- Multi-tool(Gerber #7530)
- Deluxe Hunters Pruning Kit - saw and ratcheting pruner (Gerber #46902)
- Mini Mag-Lite
- Small Game Carrier

TIP – Let's see – Hot Hands or the Camo Compact? Actually, both. The chemical hand-warmers are self-explanatory. They're cheap, they work well, and they're extremely easy to use. In fact, if you can't figure out a chemical hand-warmer, you shouldn't be in the field with a loaded gun. One more thing. I'd suggest buying either the larger (4x5) size, or the heaters designed for your toes. The big warmers, perhaps due to their larger oxygen-grabbing surface area, seem to get hotter and stay hotter longer than do the smaller ones. Likewise the toe warmers, which get hotter with less oxygen, meaning you can put one in an inside pocket, and it won't get cold before your first cup of coffee's done. The Camo Compact? I don't like to shoot with anything, e.g. a camouflage mask or net, against my face, BUT I do believe strongly in covering your face in some manner. Enter the Hunter's Specialties Camo Compact. Your choice of three, four, or five colors, along with a little mirror, and all in a small, thin snap-closure case that takes up no room whatsoever. Plus the make-up comes off easily with a little Baby Oil. Or more convenient are the small round Camo-Off pads, again from Hunter's Specialties. WARNING – Do not under any circumstances go into a Kwiki-Mart or similar convenience establishment without first removing your face paint. The folks behind the counter see plenty of weird things. Don't be one of them.

A true gentleman in every sense of the word, Tommy Akin carries an extra pair of wool socks in his bag – "just in case."

Tommy Akin – Owner, Akin Promotions, a Tennessee PR firm specializing in the outdoors

- Knight & Hale goose calls – 2 –Double Cluck Plus and the Magnum Clucker.
- Medicine bottle with extra reeds and corks
- 2 boxes of shells – #4 shot Hevi-Shot and Winchester Supreme BBs
- Avery facemask in Mossy Oak Shadow Grass
- Avery neck gaiter
- Polar-Wrap full-face mask – worn any time temperatures are 10 or colder. This is a must if you exposure your face outside the pit or blind
- 2 pairs of gloves – a pair of cotton for shooting after getting to pit, and one pair of Gore-Tex for warmth getting to pit.
- Ear Plugs – If next hunter is shooting a 10-gauge or short-barrelled gun
- Rem Oil and small rag
- Extra Avery choke tube –Open choke if geese are decoying into close range
- Choke wrench
- Leatherman tool
- Knight & Hale sunglasses – 2 pair with different color lens, one for early morning light and other for bright days
- Avery thermos bottle
- Bottle of water.
- Pair of wool socks – If I'm going where I might get wet
- Bottle of Aspirin
- Avery duck tote - They also work for geese
- Matches
- And last but certainly not least, a small roll of toilet paper

TIP – The reason folks carry a Leatherman Multi-tool lies, elementally, in the word Multi-tool. Essentially these nylon-sheathed contraptions eliminate the need for any number of different instruments, any one of which could be lost, forgotten, or flat-out ignored totally. Like most things found in blind bags across the country, Multi-tools are lightweight, compact, reliable, and rugged. And whether your intent is to poke, prod, cut, slice, dice, saw, chop, crimp, gouge, trim, shave…you get my drift…the Multi-tool will fit the bill.

"Why do guys carry Leatherman tools," says Mark Baker, head public relations man for the Portland-based company. "Goose hunting is just as gear-intensive as any other type of hunting. You have your firearms, decoys, blinds, fancy hardware. Portable heater. And if something goes wrong with any of it, there's a good chance you're saved yourself a trip back to the truck, thanks to a Leatherman."

"It's a step-saver, whether you need to adjust a hinge on a blind, re-rig a decoy, whatever," he continued. "And the time you save means more time you have for hunting."

Rod Haydel – President, Haydel Game Calls

- Nikon cool pix 5000 camera
- Olympus stylist 35mm
- Calls applicable to the hunt. – all Haydel's, duck and goose calls for different species
- Pen and paper
- Paper towels
- Leatherman
- Plastic zip ties for various emergency repairs
- Kent Tungsten Matrix #1 shot
- Haydel's DPX chokes for my gun and some extras for hunting partners to try in various thread patterns
- Haydel's Game Strap
- Batteries for cameras and extra film
- Plastic bags for any mountable prospects
- Brinkman flashlight
- Bottle of water
- Extra snuff
- Two face masks as someone always forgets one

TIP – Ah, a Zip Tie man after my own heart. Truth is, and after discovering both Zip Ties, and pop rivet guns at the age of 38, I'm reasonably sure I can build you a home, and a nice home at that, using only Zip Ties and pop rivets. In the field, Zip Ties have a million uses, so I won't even bother listing them here. Let it suffice to say that Zip Ties – various lengths, nonetheless – are a very space-saving addition to the blind bag.

Richie McKnight – Kentucky State goose calling champ (1997-2000, 2002), and winner of the 2002 US Open championship

- In an Avery Outdoors Pit Bag (Mossy Oak Shadow Grass) goes –
- Duck and goose calls by Fred Zink
- Remington Hevi-Shot, 3-inch #6
- Head light and extra batteries
- First aid kit
- Bart man lanyards
- Extra reeds and files – "I work on a lot of calls for people in the pit!"
- Extra Avery neck gaiter
- Gloves – two pair
- Avery duck totes, neoprene-covered thermos, saw and hand-cutters
- FOOD! Plenty of food

Yes, the man on the phone is indeed Richie McKnight, winner of the 2002 US Open Goose Calling Championship. Here, he's ordering out for pizza.

TIP – You'll notice that Richie, like several of the guys here, doesn't carry one pair, but rather *two pair* of gloves. Some folks, Tommy Akin for one, will carry or wear a couple different types of gloves into the field. One pair, a warm though possibly bulky set, are worn to the pit, while the other, a thinner perhaps synthetic blend, are worn during the shooting. Others, and here's where I come in, pack a couple pair just in case (1) a pair are lost in the dark during the decoy setting process, or (2) the first pair get wet, muddy, or whatever. Usually with us folk, both pair are the same – fingerless wool in my case – so there's no confusion as to which pair to wear when. Believe me, I can afford little more confusion.

Major Andrew Davis – United States Air Force, McCord Air Force Base, Washington, and avid waterfowler

- Two boxes Remington Nitro Express BBs
- Two pair of gloves (one wool)
- Facemask
- Wood *Sure Shot* goose call – Call me traditional
- Two duck calls, just in case. A *Sure Shot* 1997 Ducks Unlimited model, and an old *Mallardtone* that sounds great even when I blow it.

Scott Trienen's the only guy I know who takes *snakes* with him into the field. Read his list for the whole story. And, Scott? Sorry 'bout that.

- Full set of choke tubes with universal choke tool
- Candy bars and water
- Collapsible cleaning rod in case of mud in the barrel
- Leatherman multi-tool
- Small first aid kit

TIP – Knock on wood, I've never had occasion to use one in the field, but a small first aid kit is without question a very good idea. And who better to bring this one up than an Air Force Major. But Andy has a good point, and what's more, a compact first aid kid (1) won't take up much room, and (2) can in truth spell the difference between life and death in the field.

Scott Trienen – 2002 Minnesota State goose-calling champion and guide

- CALLS: All of these are Tim Grounds Championship Calls –
- The Hunter G 007 has a good range of volume and sounds; tuned about medium. It has that natural goosey high-pitched sound.
- Acrylic Super Mag. I have mine tuned up a little harder so that I can get the volume out of it to attract far-off geese.
- The Half-Breed. A plastic call that is tuned light. This makes it quick and high-pitched for the days

the birds want that sound. Also makes a lot of noise for small geese.
- The Long Magnum. A wooden call designed to be deeper in tone. This works great on the old refuge geese that make low, deep clucks and moans.
- A Hen Talk duck call and whistle
- Winchester Supremes and Kent Fasteel - #BB
- Modified and full choke tubes & wrench
- Can of de-icer
- Face paint
- Gloves and neoprene gloves
- Neck gaiter, face mask and stocking hat
- A game tote
- Avery snow spray
- A flashlight and compass
- Pliers, just in case the bird has some jewelry
- Snakes. You always need snakes.

Author's note: By all rights, Scott should *never* forgive me for this, but I just had to include his mention of that all-important piece of goose gear – snakes. When I first received Scott's list, I was understandably curious about this element. However, not being raised by a goose hunter and not nearly the fanatic as is Scott and the rest of this crew, I thought that perhaps *snakes* referred to some type of equipment with which I was not familiar. So what did I do? I wrote back to the boy and asked. A couple days later, I received this admittedly paraphrased response –

"M.D. Snakes? I meant snacks. You always need snacks. Man, my typing stinks." And that's one of the things I like best about this new breed, Young Gun goose hunting crowd. They're honest.

TIP – Snakes aside, the young man has some good ideas concealed inside his blind bag, the most interesting of which is a small aerosol can of lock de-icer. The same exact thing – white metal canister 'bout the size of a cigar with a little plastic tip you stick into the keyhole – that you'd use when your vehicle doors ice up. Well, it works extremely well on those bitterly cold mornings when that autoloader you're shooting refuses to cycle due to the fact that....well, let's see. You brought it in out of the cold yesterday and never bothered to take it out of the case. As the gun warmed, tiny beads of water known as condensation formed, both on the exterior as well as on the internal workings. Next morning, you take said gun out of the case and lay it in the bottom of the blind while you set the decoys. It's 20 degrees. See where I'm going with this? Either get some de-icer, or take better care of your guns.

As for me, I carry more stuff into the goose fields today than I did when I killed my first Canada in 1979. Fact is, back then, I didn't carry anything into the field except a 1966 Mossberg Model 500 – with Poly-Choke – and a handful of Federal 3-inch shotshells packed with two ounces of copper-plated #BBs. Oh, and a couple Winchester #4 buckshot rounds containing 41 pellets of some of the then deadliest goose medicine available. Or so I thought.

Nowadays, my typical load of goose gear won't fit into the pockets of my canvas Carhartt coat like it did. No, I've traded the Carhartt for a much larger and much more professional sounding *blind bag*, which, while certainly nice, offers me the opportunity to carry far too much of George Carlin's STUFF afield. But hunters are like that. Give 'em 1,512 cubic inches of storage space, not including the side and end pockets, and we'll fit something into each and every inch. But that's part of the game, isn't it?

That said, the interior of my personal blind bag looks something like this.

- Avery shell belt containing 25 rounds of 3-inch 1-⅝-ounce Hevi-Shot #2
- Handful of Winchester Supreme High Velocity #BB
- PS-Olt A-50 modified by Mike Weller
- Tim Grounds Snow/Speck call
- Fred Zink's Paralyzer SR-1 (I'm still learning)
- Randy Bartz' Flagman Flag
- Insulated camo gloves & brown toque
- Medicine/first-aid kit: Band-aids, Q-tips, safety

I took to wearing a 25-round shell belt a few years back, and today, I wouldn't want to be without it. That, and the bullets that are in it, too!

pins, cord, toilet paper, extra O-ring for 11-87
- Chemical hand-warmers
- Avery gaiter and hand-warmer
- Water bottle, snacks, and dog treats for Maggie, Jet and Deacon
- Cellular phone

TIP – I have a love/hate relationship with cell phones. I hate nothing more than to hear one ring while I'm trying to enjoy the beauty and solitude of The Wild, but, I'll admit, there are times when they can be awfully, awfully convenient. Maybe you or one of your hunting partners are injured in the field, and you need medical assistance waiting for you when you reach the ramp or the farmhouse. Or maybe it would be nice to bring down the local sheriff on the miscreants who shot into the passing flock of swans....in Iowa. Or, just maybe, your wife actually does go into labor while you're settling into the blind 15 minutes before shooting time on a field where the night before you watched 1.83 million Canadas fall into. Sorry, partner, but it's best you pack up, go home, and spend the day with the Misses. Besides, there should be time for an afternoon hunt...

Julie's Remington 11-87. A great goose gun? To some folks, yes; to others, no. That's why there are choices.

4

Great goose guns

Let me be honest with you. If there's going to be a chapter in this project wrought with controversy, debate, and outright disbelief – other, that is, than the section on calls and calling – it's going to be this one. Why do I say that?

Well, for starters, getting goose hunters to agree on the merits of a goose gun ranks right up there with trying to get a family of six to decide on what toppings they'd like on their pizza. You know exactly what I'm talking about there. Then you get into the ammunition side of things, variables such as shot size, shot composition, velocity, price – Can't forget price! – and last but certainly not least, whether the hull looks better in black, green, or red.

In all fairness, though, there are several things that make agreement on topics such as guns and ammunition difficult. One is the fact that today, there are literally dozens of excellent choices available when it comes to guns capable of killing any goose, big or small, that frequents any one of the four flyways. Some, yes, are a little more capable than others; however, when you get right down to it, it all becomes a matter of personal preference in the end. Same to some extent with ammunition, though I'd be amiss if I didn't say that there may be a greater number of mistakes to be made in choosing goose bullets as can be made deciding which goose gun to purchase. And we'll address that comment here in a bit but for now, great goose guns.

The goose gun defined

Shuffling along, under cover of night, Victor Frankenstein went about his grisly business of collecting parts. A little here and a little there. Always collecting. And then, one dark and dreary evening when the skies were violently charged with electricity, he raised his patchwork creation aloft and let Mother Nature breathe into it life.

With trembling hands, Frankenstein lowers the table and throws aside the sheet. And there, there before his unbelieving eyes, lies – the perfect goose gun.

Melodramatic? Yeah, but I couldn't resist. And actually, I do have a point. Rather, a question. What would this so-called *perfect goose gun* look like, that is if it were to become a reality? Some, I'm sure, feel that it not only already exists, but lives and breathes in their very own gun safe; however, for the sake of conversation, let's assume that such a piece doesn't exist. What would it look like? How would it function? Any of the proverbial bells and whistles?

Curious, I hunted down my own Dr. Frankenstein 2003, and asked him to describe what he'd see underneath that sheet if he did look. Chris Paradise, 35, is a diehard wingshooter and as hardcore a goose hunter as you'll find in the eastern United States. Formerly the head public relations man for Flambeau Products, Paradise now serves as senior vice-president of sales and marketing for O.F. Mossberg and Sons in North Haven, Connecticut, where, on a daily basis, he undertakes the task of making good guns even better. All that said, I asked Chris to put on his lab coat and help create, piece by piece, this ultimate goose gun. What Paradise came up was, to say the least, interesting.

Gauge – "Eight!" This is followed by much laughter, a Paradise trait that I perpetuate by constantly missing things in front of them. "A 12-gauge for me." Not the 10, I asked. "Nope. You can have the 10-gauge. Why would you shoot a 10-gauge when you can shoot the 12-gauge 3-½-inch?"

Chamber – "Three-inch. You can shoot a higher velocity load in a 3-inch load. And this gun doesn't have to be a 3½-inch. There's actually a lot faster loads in 2¾ inch, and velocity is what you need to get penetration." NOTE – More on the 3½-inch 12-gauge later.

Action – "Automatic. It's tough for me to say, pump

Regardless of the make and model, ease of maintenance, as Paradise says, is indeed important both in and out of the field.

or auto, but once I shot this new automatic (the then-new Mossberg Model 935), I never went back."

Barrel length – "Twenty-six. All day. For everything. I'll give you the whole spectrum here. A 24-inch barrel will do everything a 28-inch barrel will do. Only it doesn't give you the sight plane. So if you're a non-seasoned shooter, sometimes a 28-inch barrel will assist you. But with the advancement of choke tubes and constrictions, you can achieve the same ranges with a 24-inch as you can with a 28. Your guns are going to balance better in that 26-inch range. You can use it for turkey. You can use it for waterfowl. It's an in-between."

Porting – "No. Porting supposedly – and I say supposedly because some engineers will go back and forth on this one – reduces muzzle jump and recoil. I know what it does do, though. In a pit blind or an enclosed area with a ported gun, it blows your eardrums out."

Camouflage – "Yes. Mossy Oak's new Shadow Grass. It's awesome. But anything non-glare. Stay away from high-gloss wood. Stay away from polishes. If not camouflage, a matte finish is the best."

Chokes – "Extended ported modified. If you want to use an extended tube and put a little porting in the tube, that's fine. But as long as you have a modified tube in there, you can still run an almost full choke with steel."

Stock and fore-end – "Synthetic. No questions asked. Synthetic is going to be much more durable. These guns take a royal beating."

Weight – "From 7½ to 8½ pounds."

Sling – "Padded neoprene."

Sights – "The Fat Bead fiber optic front bead from Tru-Glo. It's a little bigger. It gathers a little more light. It's encased in metal, not plastic, so it's not going to break."

Here's where I deviated from the black-and-white variables, the actions and the gauges and so on, and pinned Paradise down on what I'll call the less elemental characteristics his creature will possess. In other words, Chris, tell me about this thing's personality.

Dependability – "It can take abuse all day long – dirt, grime, snow. It just performs."

Ease of maintenance – "It can be easily dismantled in the field. Very few pieces. This ease of maintenance thing is very important for the goose hunter."

Simplicity of design – "This great goose gun has to do two things. It's very, very simple. It needs to go *bang* when you pull the trigger, and it needs to cycle very, very efficiently. Theoretically you're shooting a lot of heavy loads – 3-inch-plus loads – with this gun, and it needs to be able to withstand that constant pounding. No bells and whistles at all."

Durability and ruggedness – "The gun we're trying to create is a gun dedicated to goose hunting. That means there could be a tornado. There could be a monsoon. There could be a blizzard. You're talking about a gun that's going to face the worst types of weather. It has to be – *has to be* – rugged and durable."

Well, does it exist? Does Doctor Paradise's creation actually live and breathe, or is it but in the minds of goose hunters across the country? True, there are, as you'll see or perhaps already know firsthand, any number of fantastic shotguns available today, any one of which might fit well the definition of a "great goose gun." However, we as hunters are always striving for something new. Something better. An extra 5 yards. Maybe 10. The ultimate goose gun. Truth is, it just might already live in your closet. Read on.

The 10-gauge: Still alive?

Remember the 16-gauge? The bastard bore – as the very proud owner of both a Remington Model 1100 and a Winchester Model 24 in 16-gauge, I hated when people called it that – that was squeezed into obscurity between the 2¾-inch 1¼-ounce 12-gauge and the 3-inch 20-gauge? Well, that one-time "gotta have it for those long shots" favorite, the 10-gauge, knows exactly what the 16 went through.

"Because of the versatility of the 3½-inch 12-gauge, we are seeing a decrease in the market for the 10-gauge; however, there continues to be a niche market for the 10, particularly among waterfowl hunters," says Linda Powell, manager of press relations for the Remington Arms Company.

Limbo. That's probably the best and most accurate way to describe the status of today's 10-gauge. But if it's true that the big 10 is but a shadow of its former self, is there then a place for the 10-gauge in modern waterfowling circles? Well, if long-range goose shooting with big, big steel pellets is a hunter's forte, then the answer might just be a resounding maybe; however, it's important to remember that the performance gap between steel and lead shot has been narrowed dramatically in recent years, thanks to a number of technological advancements in the art of ammunition making including such things as improvements in wad construction and design, and the development of high-velocity loads. In other words, it's just possible that the 3½-inch 12-gauge is, with steel, doing everything that the 10-gauge was doing, all in a lighter, more user-friendly package. Throw one of the non-toxic/non-steel ballistically superior alternatives into the mix, and the big-boy 12-gauge begins to edge out the 10 even more noticeably.

So does that mean that the handful of diehard 10-gauge fanatics out there will immediately closet their shoulder cannons and rush out to buy a replacement 3½-inch 12? Is Jacobs Field empty on a Saturday afternoon in June just because the Cleveland Indians haven't won a pennant since 1948? I don't think so.

Some 3-inch, and some 3.5-inch. From left to right – Julie's Beretta AL390, Benelli Super Black Eagle, Benelli Nova, Remington 11-87, and Mossberg 835.

New kid on the block: The 3½-inch 12-gauge

I hope I don't embarrass him, but if I were told to pick a man to sit next to me in a goose pit, someone that I had to rely on to be a predator. To make shot after shot after impossible shot, and do it with a look in his eye that makes me think – "Damn, I'm glad I'm not a goose" – that man would be L.P. Brezny. Now living in the Black Hills of South Dakota, Brezny, who some of you may also know as the shotgunning editor for *Wildfowl* magazine, has over the past 30 years expended more shotgun ammunition than most of us will ever see. Let alone fire. And while a goodly portion of these shotshells have been fired at a pattern board or through a chronograph, Brenzy has shot at enough living feathered things, geese included, to more than justify his title of "shotgun performance evaluator."

And so it was with this all in mind that I called Brenzy one afternoon at his home in the Hills, and asked him very simply – "What's up with the 3½-inch 12-gauge?"

"Volume for shot size," said Brezny. "That's why it exists. It came into existence primarily for steel shot. Anything else (NOTE: shot material, that is) is pretty much irrelevant. But for steel shot, as pellet size increased, volume was lost. And the 3-inch 12 just didn't have the

The Mossberg 835, a 3.5-inch gun that will handle all the 3-inch stuff you want to stuff in it…and then some.

capacity. So in order to up the shot size and maintain the pellet count, which essentially is volume and capacity, the 3½ was developed. Specifically."

But isn't this 3½-inch 12-gauge, I asked L.P., in truth a redundancy when you look at a 3½-inch 10-gauge? "Apples and oranges," said Brezny, with no hesitation whatsoever. "Apples and oranges."

"The 10-gauge is the 10-gauge, essentially at all levels. You can't do anything with it, simply because it's a big, unwieldy 10-gauge. The beauty of the 3½-inch 12, and it was almost a secondary benefit that happened by accident, is the fact that it was found to be extremely flexible. How so? Well, you can go down to a 2½-inch English (shotshell) in it, if you want to. You can buy an X2 or a Gold or an 11-87, whatever your fancy is, and you can go out and shoot a round of trap with it. And then the next weekend, you can go out and pound Canadas off a pass line with it," said Brezny.

All right. So the 3½-inch 12-gauge was a creature born of the steel shot revolution. A thing of necessity. Understood; however, with advancements in shot technology – Hevi-Shot, bismuth, tungsten-iron, and the like – hasn't, then, the 3½-inch 12-gauge outlived its usefulness as a goose gun? I mean, can't we simply go back to shooting our traditional 3-inch 12s loaded with these high-performance, though admittedly spendy, modern shotshells? Brezny's answer was immediate.

"No," said Brezny, "simply because it's (the 3½-inch 12-gauge) badly needed in the steel shot market. And the steel shot market will still always be king because of economics. It's a price point issue. And the fact that the new steel shot is extremely good. The old stuff of five years ago can't hold a candle to today's steel, and the stuff from 10 years ago is like a Model T."

Keeping in mind L.P. Brezny's – "The 3½-inch 12-gauge still very much has a role" – comment, the obvious question then centers around the relevancy of the traditional 3-inch 12, particularly for those goose hunters who either won't or can't shoot the expensive non-steel alternatives. Basically, does the 3-inch 12 still have a place in the blind or the pit?

"The 3-inch 12-gauge is still a contender, as they say, but the 3½-inch 12 does give you that extra edge. It does turn that corner when you need a little more horsepower. When you're sitting up there on the Missouri River and you're working off the bluffs. Or you're working Rochester, Minnesota, and they're just *not* cooperating with that last five or 10 yards that you really need. When you're right on that ballistic edge and you need that little sweet spot in the pattern, that's the 3½-inch 12-gauge."

He continued. "How do the two compare? Shot size for shot size, it's no contest because the 3½-inch is going to be throwing more shot. It's just a bigger kid in the alley. No matter how you cut it. It's going to throw a bigger payload at relatively the same velocity."

Old reliable: The 3-inch 12

L.P.'s right. You really can't compare the 3½-inch 12-gauge to the 3-inch when you're talking BBs to BBs. It's like weighing the carrying capacity of your old Radio Flyer wagon against that of an ox cart. As Brezny says, it's no contest.

So, does this mean that as a big pellet-throwing goose gun, the 3-inch 12-gauge is, for all intents and purposes, deceased?

"It seems like everyone wants to shoot the 3½-inch, or at least have that 3½-inch capability," said Phil Bourjaily, shooting editor for *Field & Stream*. Each year, Bourjaily shoots a ton, and did so long before he earned his official title with the folks in New York City. He's also an avid waterfowler, and one of the few non-fanatics I know who would rather hunt geese than he would ducks. So it was with these qualities in mind that I called him to ask about the current heart rate of the once-so-popular 3-inch 12-gauge.

"But, that said, there are still plenty of situations where a 3-inch gun is every bit the equal of a 3½, especially when you start looking at the premium non-toxic shots. The 3½-inch 12-gauge (NOTE: Remember Brezny?) was invented in order to allow hunters to get lots of big steel pellets, which are not only big but light, into a hull. And now with things like Hevi-Shot, bismuth, and tungsten…these things don't need to be put into a 3½-inch hull in order to get something that kills geese," he continued.

Does this mean, I asked my friend, that the hunter dead set on sticking with his 3-inch 12-gauge should give serious consideration to turning away from steel and going with one of these new so-called "premium non-toxics?"

"Yeah," said Bourjaily, somewhat hesitantly. "But I wouldn't overlook the 3-inch High Velocity BB load. That's 1¼ ounces of steel BBs going 1,450 feet per second. And it's a tremendous goose killer. Plus, if you look at the numbers, I think the 3½-inch hull will have, like, nine more pellets in it. So I don't know how much more killing power that adds up to. These High Velocity 3-inch BB loads are great for geese over decoys, out to 40 yards, or anywhere you don't need the absolute high-end pellet count."

"That said, when you get into Hevi-Shot, which is heavier than lead, you can use smaller pellets than you would with steel and get more of 'em in a smaller hull, then a 3-inch, or even a 2¾ inch gun, is more than enough to hold more than enough pellets to kill geese as far away as anyone should be shooting at them. It's almost the same with bismuth or with Kent's Tungsten-Matrix, which is great stuff. Of course, all of these manufacturers load a 3½-inch hull because everyone thinks that if 3-inch is

Confidence begins at the patterning board. Here, Phil Bourjaily checks the results of just one of many rounds fired this particular afternoon.

good, then 3½ must be better. The way I look at it? How dead is dead?"

But it was what Bourjaily said next that made perhaps the most sense to me as to why the 3-inch 12-gauge is certainly *not* out of the running as a fine goose gun.

"Three inch guns will cycle really light loads much better than will a 3½. This means that I can take my 3-inch gun to the skeet field or the trap range or the sporting clays course during the spring and summer, and shoot the same gun in practice as I'll be shooting for geese in the fall. This, without having to shoot heavier practice loads or having to worry about whether or not the gun's going to cycle properly. That's why I prefer the 3-inch guns," said Bourjaily.

Myself? I'll cut right to the chase here. I shoot 3-inch 12-gauge shotshells, regardless of whether or not the gun I'm shooting handles the next size larger. Why do it shoot 3-inch? Four reasons –

Confidence – I have all the confidence in the world in myself and my primary goose guns, which include a Remington 11-87 and a Mossberg Model 935. This confidence is the result of field experience, as well as each firearm's consistent performance on the patterning board. Too, and as Bourjaily just mentioned, I'm able to shoot both of these guns quite often during the summer with either light field loads, or better yet, Winchester's low-recoil target loads, and in doing so maintain my 'eye' for opening day. Practice breeds confidence, and confidence,

Mossberg's newest child, the Model 935 3.5-inch autoloader. To date, mine's been a fine performer in the field, as has Phil Bourjaily's pictured here.

as you know, is the main ingredient in success.

Ammunition – While I agree completely with L.P. Brezny's assessment of the 3½ 12-gauge being the "bigger kid in the alley," I also agree with Bourjaily's comment concerning how today's "premium" non-toxic 3-inch ammunition has helped level the playing field. For geese, I shoot Winchester's High Velocity BBs or Remington's Hevi-Shot #2s, either one of which, I feel, has not only evened the teams, but have helped make me a better shooter and hunter through such things as self-restraint, more efficient use of decoys and calls, and more accurate range estimation. And what role do these variables play in the 3-inch scheme of things? Get 'em close, and kill 'em dead.

Pain – Why beat a bug with a railroad tie when a fly-swatter will work just fine? No, the 3½-inch goose guns aren't that bad, although Patterning Day will certainly leave its mark on you; still, the older I get, the less I like to get abused by inanimate objects such as shotguns. That's what editors are for.

Self-discipline – Yes, and finally, self-discipline. Let me put it this way, and some, will disagree; however, I'll say it nonetheless. If a goose is so far away that I can't kill it with a 3-inch 12-gauge shotshell containing 1¼ ounces of High Velocity steel BBs or 1⅝ ounces of Hevi-Shot #2s, then I shouldn't be shooting at it with anything.

Everything else

Certainly there will be folks out there who disagree, some adamantly, when I say that anything short of a heavy 2¾ inch 12-gauge makes a poor offering in the goose fields. True, I've killed Canadas with two different 16-gauge pieces; however, and as much as I love both the Model 1100 and the Model 24 double that reside in the closet, I wouldn't rank either of them very high on the "Great Goose Guns" scale. Certainly, advancements in shotshell technology, e.g. Hevi-Shot, bismuth, tungsten-matrix, and High-Velocity loads, have helped move the modern 16-gauge a bit more into the realm of the water-fowler. The key words here? *A* and *bit*. Perhaps some capable shooters still carry the 16-gauge, with its non-toxic loads of one or 1⅛ ounces of #4 steel or #5 bismuth, into the duck marsh, but you'll find few – damn few – 16s, in the goose pit of 2004. Why? It's simple. You can't cram enough big steel pellets – BBB, BB; or #1 minimum – into a 16-gauge hull. Handloading Hevi-Shot #2s into a 16-gauge hull and gunning 25 to 30-yard Canadas over decoys? Well, now we're talking about something altogether different. That I'd go with. But very few people will do it.

The 3-inch 20-gauge? Day in and day, under normal goose hunting conditions, the 20-gauge, like the 16, probably wouldn't get the nod as a goose gun. Yes, even in the 3-inch version. There are factory goose-like loads available for the 3-inch 20, with Federal rolling a hull containing an ounce of steel #1 (103 pellet count), as well as one holding ⅞-ounce of tungsten-iron #2 (approximately 90 pellets); still, and even with these, you'll need almost optimum, over-decoys conditions for any type of consistency. If you have those kind of conditions, *and* the self-discipline and experience to combine with the limitations of the 3-inch 20-gauge throwing non-toxics, then I say more power to you. Or, if you're one of those who enjoys hand-loading, we can always fall back on the aforementioned ounce of Hevi-Shot #2 in the 20-gauge hull. As with the 16-gauge shooting the same rounds, I'd be all right with that. For the most part, though, when you get down to the 20-gauge, you begin to run into the same problem you did with the 16. Not enough room.

And finally, the 28-gauge and .410. Don't laugh. I understand that there are indeed those who use them, and quite efficiently, for not only geese, but sandhill cranes and swans as well. I hear tell of a gentleman out West who handloads 28-gauge and .410 shotshells. Fills them with steel #7 or Hevi-Shot #7½ and picks his shots very, very carefully. The loads, I'm told, have undergone extensive ballistics testing, not to mention a hell of a lot of time spent in front of a patterning board. And then there's the countless hours in the field; however, my point is this – While, yes, in extremely skilled hands and with tirelessly crafted handloads, the 28 and .410 will work for geese, the

Okay, so it's not a Super Mag; however, this 1988-vintage 11-87 (3-inch) carries itself quite well in the goose fields.

chances are also very good that you'll hunt your entire life-time and never – NEVER – come across one in use in the goose field. Part of it, you might agree, is the American mentality of *Big Guns for Big Things*. And I'm not so sure that in the case of something as tenacious of life as a 15-pound Canada goose, this big equals big way of thinking isn't a good idea.

Some of the favorites

Now here's where things start to get really interesting, the point at which I pull but a handful of feathers out of the entire feather pillow. And the point at which some readers out there will slam their fist down on the counter and stammer – "Well, of all the…! This goofball has absolutely no idea what he's talking about!!"

What I'm talking about, just in case you missed the feathers and pillow analogy, are not only great goose guns, but favorite great goose guns. The ones that for one reason or another outshine all the others. Those modern firearms that if you were to round up any 100 pit-sitters on any given day during the season, a good 75 percent of them would be carrying one of the following. Knowing I run of risk of lighting the flame under that ever-smoldering tabletop argument – "Mine's better, and here's why! NO, mine's better, and I'm gonna tell you why!!" – these are simply some of the finest. Or more precisely, some of the favorites.

Mossberg Model 835 – Introduced in 1988 as the first shotgun to be offered in a 3½-inch chamber. And the rest, as the cliché goes, is history. The Model 835 exhibits, as does its older 3-inch brother, the Model 500 (1961), all those qualities that make a shotgun a great goose gun; however, where the 835, again like the 500, excels is in the realm of dependability and durability. Hunting the Columbia River estuary – translation: saltwater – for late-season Canadas? Not a problem for the 835. Same thing on the East Coast. Same thing in the Texas salt marshes or a muddy Missouri cornfield. You want something rugged? Something you can use as an oar or that will pull double-duty as a tire iron, only to be hosed down and go imme-diately back into service from the pit? Well, sir, you're going to be hard-pressed to find something that will best the 835. No, there's no fancy engraving. And, no, chances are you won't impress the next guy with what you paid for your Model 835. But you shoot it well and it goes BOOM each and every time you pull the trigger, now doesn't it? What more do you need?

As for the **Mossberg Model 500**, same story – dependable, rugged, strong, and reliable. No fashion state-ment with this one, but then again, the words *second mort-gage* won't enter the picture either. I know. I've said it before, but I killed my first Canada – my first goose – with a vintage 1966 Model 500. And my first red fox. And my first gray squirrel. And one of my first mallards. If you think about it, you probably did too. That's part of the rea-

I absolutely fell in love with the Winchester Super X2. It comes apart easily, never hiccups, and eats…and spits out…whatever you put in it. Who could ask for more?

son why it's here under Favorites.

And finally, Mossberg's new **Model 935**. I had an opportunity to stand behind one of Mossberg's new 3½ autoloaders in September of 2003 as part of a pick-up goose and dove hunt in the northeast corner of Ohio that the Paradise Brothers, Chris and Rob, had put together, and as far as an autoloader retailing for $400 was concerned, I was impressed. My initial concern was that there were a lot of guts, aka internal parts, which there are; however and despite this plethora 'o parts, the gun is relatively simple in design as well as assembly and disassembly, and during the two days we tested the quartet of then-new 935s, there was never a problem. Yes, it failed to reliably cycle 2¾ inch shotshells, but Mossberg never intended nor claimed the Model 935 to be a 2¾ through 3½-inch gun. So, if you're looking for a traditional Mossberg-quality autoloader that will eat and spit out 3 and 3½-inch bullets AND won't ravage your wallet, the Model 935 certainly does deserve a look.

Remington Model 11-87 Super Magnum – I bought my first 11-87 in October of 1988. Chris Kirby of Quaker Boy Game Calls had invited me to central New York to hunt Canadas, and I wanted something new. Something different. Remington autoloaders were no stranger to me. I'd shot a 16-gauge Model 1100 since 1979, and absolutely loved the way they performed in the field – reliable, easy to maintain. And for whatever reason, I shot them well. Sixteen years and literally thousands of rounds later, the

1988 Model 11-87 still has its original O-ring, and has accounted for scores of geese from Louisiana to Manitoba and from Washington's Pacific Coast to New York state…and a bunch of places in-between. Complaints? None at all. As a goose getter, I'd rank it well into the Top Five, along with its more recent and slightly larger cousin, the 3½-inch **11-87 Super Magnum**. Yes, the gas-metering system in the Super Magnum has been changed somewhat in order that the mechanics can compensate for the pressure differences between light 2¾ inch field loads and these huge honking 3½-inch goose loads so popular today; still, it's the same old Model 11-87 that was introduced some 17 years back.

Should I mention the **Remington Model 870 Super Magnum**? For many hunters, waterfowlers or no, not to mention the Model 870 pump would be a travesty. An insult. Is there a reason why the Model 870 is the best-selling pump-gun on the market today? Actually, there are several, and they're all listed under "The Goose Gun Defined." Like the Mossberg Model 500, the Remington 870 Super Magnum has it all – and a 3½-inch chamber to boot. I don't think I'll get much argument on this count. The Model 870, 3-inch or 3½, belongs here.

Winchester Super X2 – I shot Winchester's Super X2 autoloader during the whole of the 2002-2003 season, as well as for the better portion of the 2003-04 season, and frankly, I was impressed. Mostly 3-inch shotshells, mind you, but on those few occasions I fed her what she was

50

That's a black synthetic Super Black Eagle, or SBE, in the background that Christian Curtis is shooting. To many, there is *no other* goose gun.

designed for, the 3½-inch hull, the Super X2 functioned without so much as a hiccup, belch, or backfire. From Canada – twice, and lots of rounds – to Washington, Iowa, Ohio, Arkansas, Nebraska, and southern Illinois, everything was as it should be; that is, reliable, dependable, and easy to maintain.

Benelli Super Black Eagle – While the gun was introduced in its now-famous 3½-inch form in 1991, it wasn't until 1993, or maybe 1994, that I witnessed the hub-bub that this Shotgun of Shotguns caused among waterfowling circles in western Washington. Whispered conversations at the 16-yard line at the Evergreen Sportsman's Club – "Did you see it?" one would ask. "See it! Hell, I touched it." And farther on down the line – "Touched it! I know a guy whose friend actually shot one." And thus the Pacific Northwest met, and fell in love with, the Benelli Super Black Eagle, or SBE, the nation's first 3½-inch autoloader.

Since its introduction, the SBE has taken the country by storm. A most reliable semi-auto, the SBE features an inertia-driven operating system as opposed to the more commonly seen gas-operated machines. Translation? The SBE pushes most of the powder residue, dirt, and grime associated with high-volume fire out the muzzle, NOT into the guts of the gun. The result? A cleaner gun internally that's a snap to maintain and will continue belching those big 3½-inch goose-killer rounds out just as long as you're pulling the trigger.

"The inertia system is far cleaner than the gas-operated systems," said Steve McKelvain, director of brand marketing and communications for Benelli USA. "And with this lack of a gas system, you don't have the fouling mixing with water and ice and the gunk commonly found in goose hunting situations. The Super Black Eagle is a simple system, with only seven parts to the bolt mechanism. Because of this simplicity, you don't have a lot of complicated linkages to mess with. No O-rings. This system, too, makes for a better balanced gun than the gas-operated systems which have all the working parts up in the forearm."

McKelvain continued. "People do want the versatility that the Super Black Eagle offers. The 2¾, 3-inch, and the 3½-inch. But what appeals to the waterfowler is the fact that you can shoot it all day in very adverse weather conditions, and it'll still function. We had one guy tell us that his action actually iced up – rain running down the barrel and into the action froze up – and he poured hot coffee down it and got it working. Not that we'd recommend doing that."

My experience with the **Benelli Nova** has been limited to portions of two seasons. A friend of mine calls it the Darth Vader gun because of the shotgun's new-fangled one-piece stock and receiver and its somewhat futuristic appearance. However, all of that time was spent under what I would consider grueling conditions on the Lower Columbia River near the Washington Coast. Sand, saltwater, weeds, mud, sleet. You name it and the Nova had it

Today's non-toxic shotshells are a far cry from what we started with in the 1980s; however, selection doesn't always make the choice easy. Find what works for you and your shotgun.

thrown at it – or was thrown into it. And through it all, a quick wipe-down with an equally sloppy sleeve, and the gun was back in action. No stuttering. No stumbling. Just shootin' and shuckin', and shootin' some more. Classic looks? No. Traditional lines? No? Strong, reliable goose gun capable of regurgitating anything you throw in it, and doing it time after time after time? Yep.

"When the Nova came out," said McKelvain, "there were people who either loved it or hated it. But then, even the guys who didn't like the non-traditional look of it saw how it functioned. They saw the ergonomics of it and the way it was designed all had a purpose behind it. So the Nova's become…well, it's like the Super Black Eagle. As far as pumps go, they've been around for years, but all the pumps that are out there now, other than the Nova, are relying on technology that's 50 years old or older."

"The Nova," he continued, "presented a way of making a pump with superior functionality and dependability. And as a waterfowl specific gun, it's very weather resistant, what with the polymer stock and the polymer encased cage inside the receiver. Overall, the Nova's really caught on, and we find that we have a tiger by the tail here. We're selling boatloads of 'em."

Selecting shotshells

I'm going to say this just for the sake of nostalgia. I killed my first goose back in 1979 with two ounces of cop-

There's a lot more to choke tubes than just picking one that says *Goose Tube*, slapping it in your shotgun, and hitting the field. This section is a must-read.

per-plated BBs. Lead BBs. At the time, pre-1991, it was my favorite goose load. Yes, sir. Two 3-inch rounds of copper BBs backed by another 3-inch hull containing 41 pellets of #4 buckshot. Also lead. Talk about performance. It was awesome.

Those days, as most of you know and those who don't soon will, are over now. Actually, they ended in 1991 when the U.S. Fish and Wildlife Service mandated that all waterfowl hunting be conducted with federally-approved non-toxic ammunition. Shot, that is. The change, at first, was difficult to say the least. Some waterfowlers quit altogether, citing justifiable reasons ranging from the price of the new ammunition to potential firearm damage and, as if any more were necessary, the plain and simple fact that this new material, these new steel shotshells, didn't perform worth a damn. And they didn't. Those that hung in there – well, they made adjustments. Some bought new shotguns. Some, and I include myself here, began to shorten their traditional shooting distances. "The days of 100-yard shots are over now," the man told my father and me the night before the opener, oh-so-many moons ago. Truthfully, I never knew that football field shots were ever around the goose fields – lead, steel, or kryptonite – but regardless, we started to discipline ourselves. And, with practice, we eventually became more adept at shooting and killing with this new material, steel.

Fortunately, the past decade and a half has brought about tremendous – and that's an understatement – changes in steel shotshells. Better powders and more efficient wad designs have lead to higher velocities and heightened performance, both on the patterning board and in the field. The introduction of the aforementioned 3.5-inch 12-gauge has afforded goose hunters the luxury of not only increased pellet counts, but increased counts *with* larger pellets. And perhaps most significantly, we as waterfowlers have adapted to the limitations that steel brings to the table. We have educated ourselves. We've practiced our craft until we're confident with this new ammunition. And, when the dust had all settled and tradition arose wearing little more than a grass stain and a slightly blackened eye, we came to grips with the simple fact that this was the way it was going to be. It was, we were told, steel or nothing. And I for one didn't like the sound of that word – nothing.

Staying with steel

Let me preface this particular segment by saying that, yes, I do realize that there are available non-toxic alternatives to steel shot which are comparable or, lest I say it, better than lead shot ever was, and we'll get to those in a minute; however, for the time being, let's take a quick look at the 21st century's version of steel shotshells, and the technological advancements that have contributed to the fact that these steel loads still rank a place in today's goose pit. Or at least they do in the opinions of many, myself included.

1. The 3.5-inch hull. This one's easy, as the 3.5-inch hull simply allows a greater number of larger steel pellets to be crammed into the shotshell itself and, ultimately, out the muzzle and in the general direction of a goose. This is a good thing, for with the exception of close-quarters shooting and even then, goose hunters want the energy transfer offered by large pellets AND the pattern density that comes with a high pellet count.

Enter – the 3.5-inch hull.

2. Improved powders and wads. Another easy one to understand. Better burning, more efficient powders lend themselves to consistency, which in turn aids in improved patterns. Advancements in powders, as well as primers, have also contributed to increases in muzzle velocity, a factor we'll discuss here shortly. Likewise, wads and wad design in terms of steel shotshells have both been upgraded, and both, as makes sense, relate directly back to patterns and consistency. It's a circular thing, to be sure, but one that does benefit those of us who still shoot steel.

3. Choke tubes designed specifically for steel. Here's a good one. I figured that the choke tubes out there designed specifically for steel shot and with the waterfowler in mind had to be, well, beneficial to the man shooting steel shot. "Hype," says Rob Roberts of the Arkansas-based Ballistic Specialties (800-276-2550). "It's great marketing. You can shoot the same choke for steel as you do for lead; however, if you're shooting an improved modified for lead and you shoot steel through it, it's then more of a *full* choke simply because there's no give to steel." Roberts continued by saying that while today's waterfowl-specific choke tubes may look different, with their catchy names, knobs, knurls, cuts, and ports – NOTE: Ported choke tubes do nothing to reduce recoil or muzzle jump, a misunderstood concept to many according to Roberts. Ported barrels, on the other hand, can. – they're all made of the same material (17-4 stainless steel) and differ only in constriction or inside diameter. Conversely, a tube created specifically *for an individual gun*, such as is done by the folks at Ballistics, will be truly matched not only to that individual barrel, but to the shotshells AND the situation, e.g. #1 steel at geese over decoys (25-35 yards) which will be used and encountered, respectively. "Here's what I'd tell you to do once we have your barrel here," suggested Roberts, whose outfit can turn a barrel around in two to three days. "I'd lengthen and polish the forcing cone. You're going to have less recoil and better patterns with that. There's not a downside to it. We'll then mic (measure the inside diameter of the barrel using a micrometer) the barrel. Say the bore diameter is .728, and you say you want shoot BBs at geese and #2s at ducks. I'd say go with a $^{15}/_{1000}$ constriction for your #2s, and a $^{25}/_{1000}$ constriction for your longer range stuff." All these improvements, *plus* two custom-built tubes for $195. Not a bad deal when you think

Fitted with an *H.S. Waterfowl .715* choke, this Mossberg M935 works best with Winchester's 3-inch High Velocity #BBs – a fact uncovered on the range and proved in the field.

you can pay $80 or more for a "waterfowl choke" that won't do any more than your factory modified tube, eh?

4. Better pellets. Okay, so not much has been done with the actual pellets themselves. "It's the propellants. It's the speed. It's the components. It's all those things," said Linda Barnhart, sales manager for Kent Cartridge (888-311-KENT) in Kearneysville, West Virginia. "Steel is steel, and there's not much you can do to change that. It still has the same density. It still has the same weight. The pellets still have the same diameter. But it's the combination of things, once you put that same steel in that new wad in that new hull with that new powder and a new primer, that makes it become more effective in today's application." That said, Barnhart reminds folks that not all guns are steel-friendly, a trait that's true particularly with the older model shotguns; however, manufacturers, Kent included, have addressed this concern as you'll see in just a bit.

5. High-velocity steel ammunition. Velocity means energy, energy means penetration, and penetration means improved on-target performance. And all this means one thing – more geese dead…stone dead…in the air. Standard velocity steel will average, say, 1,300 feet per second (fps); high-velocity ammunition, on the other

hand, will exit the muzzle at 1,450 to 1,550 fps, depending on the load and the manufacturer. Sure there'll be a little bigger *push* on your end of the gun, but the difference this stuff makes is more than worth the shove.

6. Price. Let's face it. The fact that you can today find quality steel shotshells, and by that I mean quality goose loads, at a price damn near comparable to lead is very attractive to a lot of folks, myself included. Certainly, some of these budget bullets won't read Winchester, Remington, or Federal, names we've come to know, love, and trust; however, some will, as each of the Big Three currently manufacture and market good non-toxic shotshells that won't ravage your wallet. You still have to determine which rounds work best out of your particular fowling piece, but at $10-$12 per 25-round box…well, that certainly does lend itself well to experimentation, eh?

So, with that all said, what do I shoot when I'm shooting steel at geese? Well, I've been through most, and have settled on Winchester's Supreme High-Velocity Super Steel, otherwise known as the Big Black Bullets. More specifically, I'm shooting a 1¼ ounce shot charge in a 3-inch 12 at 1,450 fps. Shot size? BBs, unless it's an in-your-face kind of situation over decoys, and then I'll opt for the pattern density and multiple on-target hits afforded by #2 steel. Same shot charge, same velocity, same everything, just more, slightly smaller pellets. Oh, and all out of a standard issue, from-the-factory modified RemChoke.

Something other than steel

Okay, so here's where it gets interesting. While modern steel shotshells have simultaneously increased in performance *and* decreased in price dramatically over the past five years, that same time frame has seen incredible advances in shotshell technology. Or more precisely, advances in that which fills the hulls – the shot itself. With that in mind, let's take a short look at what is available to the goose hunter in the world known as both non-toxic AND non-steel –

Remington's Hevi-Shot – If you haven't heard by now…well, you've obviously been residing under the proverbial rock. Formerly known as Environ-Metal, Inc., of Albany, Oregon, Hevi-Shot ammunition is now being manufactured and offered by the good folks at Remington Arms. Same high brass ribbed green hull that we all grew up with; however, today, that case is filled with something just a little bit different than the #2 lead pellets we used to use for geese. A mixture of oddly-shaped pellets comprised of 50 percent tungsten, 35 percent nickel, and 15 percent iron, to be precise. Hevi-Shot's claim to fame rests on the statement that it's denser than lead, which it is – lead's 11.2 grams per cubic centimeter versus 12 grams/per for Hevi-Shot (HS). What's this hodgepodge of numbers mean? Well, gone is the "two shot sizes bigger in steel than lead" rule of thumb of yesterday; in fact, gunners can now safely drop a full shot size when using Hevi-Shot, e.g. #4 HS for #2 *lead*, and lose almost nothing in terms of per-pellet downrange energy while dramatically increasing pellet count and, therefore, pattern density. For this I can vouch personally.

So, is there a downside to this better-than-lead non-toxic alternative? If there were, it would have to be price – Hevi-Shot today retails for from $1.50 to $2 per bullet; however, Hevi-Shot is available in bulk for those who would wish to fill their own green hulls with these intriguing little BBs, an answer to those who might cringe at the price while drooling at the product.

My pet load in Hevi-Shot for geese? Myself, I'm both conservative in my shooting distances *and* a huge fan of pattern density; therefore, you'll find me loaded up with 3-inch 12-gauge hulls containing 1½ ounce of HS #2, which seems more than sufficient for birds out to 40 yards and slightly beyond. Key word – slightly. My only change? Over decoys, I'll occasionally downsize and shoot 1½ ounces of HS #4, which throws as devastatingly dense a pattern as you would ever need.

The Federal Cartridge Company – The Federal Cartridge Company, a subsidiary of ATK Ammunition and Related Products, offers waterfowlers a choice of metallurgic combinations including tungsten-polymer, tungsten-iron, and tungsten-iron/steel, the last being interestingly layered loads consisting of either #2 steel shot over-top a foundation of #4 tungsten-iron, or steel BBs over tungsten-iron #2. From a density standpoint, you don't have an equal here as compared to Hevi-Shot. It's close, but not the same; therefore, I'm looking at a tungsten-iron or tungsten-poly shot in #2 over decoys, and the same material, only BBs, for anything that even remotely approaches long-distance.

The Bismuth Cartridge Company – Next to lead on the periodic table of elements, bismuth provides a much heavier alternative than does steel, the shot being comprised of 97 percent bismuth and 3 percent tin. When the ammunition was first introduced in 1995 as both a federally approved non-toxic and an "old gun" friendly material, I shot quite a bit of it and was quite impressive with its performance on geese as well as ducks and upland birds. Since the introduction of Hevi-Shot and some of the improved steel products, however, I've personally gotten away from the Bismuth No-Tox, though the folks there

The nicest thing about bismuth is that it's "old gun" friendly, a good thing to those who can't part with those 3-inch 12 side-by-sides.

certainly do continue to cater to the shotgunning community – goose hunters included.

"The difference between bismuth and all the other non-toxic alternatives," says Dan Flaherty, director of marketing for the company, "is that bismuth is soft like lead, and you can shoot it in any gun without fear of damaging the barrel or barrels. And because it is soft like lead, it upsets (NOTE: Deforms) when it hits a target, and doesn't go right through like some of the alternatives."

Of interesting note is the fact that The Bismuth Cartridge Company is the only North American company making non-toxic ammunition for all of the standard gauges and calibers, as well as some not-so-standard bores. "We have .410 through 10-gauge, including a 2½-inch 12-gauge and the 10-gauge 2⅞-inch shotshells. We're not a big company, but we try to give people what they want."

As of this writing, the company offers goose hunters their choice of 3 or 3½-inch 12-gauge high-velocity (1,375 fps) shotshells packing 1⅜- and 1⅝-ounce charges, respectively, of BBs, #2, #4, or #5 shot, as well as a 10-gauge 3½-inch HV round also throwing 1⅜ ounces of BBs through #4s. Standard velocity (1,225-1,250 fps) 3-inch 12-gauge and 3½-inch 12 and 10-gauge loads containing 1⅝- and 1⅞-ounce charges of BBs through #4s are also available.

Kent Cartridge Company – Among today's waterfowling crowd, the folks at the Kent Cartridge Company

It's all about practice, confidence, and knowing what that shotgun's going to do EVERY time you pull the trigger.

are perhaps best known for their high-velocity steel offering called, simply, Kent FASTEEL. Running upwards of 1,550 to 1,560 fps, FASTEEL has earned itself a following from coast to coast, and with good reason. In its BBB, BB and even #1 shot size format, FASTEEL is potent goose medicine regardless of whether the targets are 4-pound cacklers or 14-pound giants.

But this section is all about *non-steel* non-toxics. Well, Kent Cartridge has that option covered too, thanks to their IMPACT tungsten matrix ammunition.

Here, the word *matrix* simply means a mixture of powdered tungsten and polymers, or nylon, in amounts designed to approximate lead in density and performance. Over the course of the past two seasons, I've been very impressed with the performance of these IMPACT shotshells, not only for waterfowl, but for upland birds as well. Unfortunately, the largest shot size available in the IMPACT line is #1 – great stuff for geese over decoys, but some would feel a bit small for anything beyond, say, 45 yards.

5

Decoys: The art of deception

"A goose hunter without decoys is just another guy who gets up w-a-a-a-y too early."

Save for the pass-shooter, decoys have become as much a part of the goose hunting experience as are the birds themselves.

Yes, it is a cliché, but goose hunting and decoys go together just like major league baseball and $6 cups of lukewarm beer. Certainly, you can kill birds, and in some cases quite consistently, without decoys – See pass-shooting in Chapter 9 – but for the vast majority of the nation's goose hunters, and here I think I'd be safe in saying about 98 percent…well, goose hunting just isn't goose hunting without at least a dozen, give or take 1,000, fake Canadas, snows, specks, or what-have-you.

By way of introducing this particular chapter, I'll step out of character and be brief. The theory behind goose decoys is absolutely no different today than it was when primitive man, hungry for something other than roots and

berries, twisted a clump of cattails into a shape only vaguely resembling a goose, covered it with feathers from a coyote kill, and put it at the edge of a prehistoric swamp. There he waited, extra-full choked club in hand, for an unsuspecting bird to venture near this fraudulent companion goose. W-h-a-c-k! And with a quick blow, he had not only a meal, but plenty of feathers with which to coat his future creations. Before long, and aided greatly by the invention of the wheel, this early waterfowler was hauling 15 dozen cattail-and-feather decoys out to the fields adjacent the swamp, all on the off-chance he'd whack another main course. And the rest, they say, is history.

But while their purpose has not changed at all over the past several centuries, goose decoys have undergone

Lightweight space-savers, silhouettes are great either by themselves or as fillers used in among other types of decoys.

quite the transformation. Gone are the fragile feather-covered tufts of native vegetation. Missing too, or at least for the most part, are the wonderfully hand-carved wooden Canadas, snows, swans, and brant that graced the waters of Chesapeake Bay, the Mississippi, and the Sacramento Valley during the 19th and in the early days of the 20th centuries. Today, and while some continue to cling to the old ways and the old materials, plastics have replaced the wood and the cork and the paper mache' almost entirely. Rugged, resistant, and easy to maintain, plastic goose decoys, be they hard plastic or flexible, have become the standard among goose hunters. And with each passing season, it seems as though these plastic geese become more and more realistic. Some, spawned from hand-carved molds, are airbrushed down to the smallest detail. Others are actually photographic replicas, each one as difficult to tell from the real thing as would a Xerox copy of a Canada. Others move – a shimmy here, a wiggle there. A spin, a twist, a turn, and a flap, each intended to fool the eyes as well as the hunters' calls fool the ears. Or at least it's supposed to work that way.

And that's really the bottom line as far as decoys are concerned, this fooling the eyes. "It's an illusion," experienced hunters like Brad Harris have told me on more than one occasion. "All these calls and decoys; it's just all part of the illusion. You're making it appear safe. You make it sound real. And with decoys, you make it look natural." If the decoys could talk, they might say, "Nothing wrong down here. Nothing amiss. Come on down and grab a bite. And pay no attention to the man behind the curtain. I've seen him shoot."

The many faces of decoys

All right. So now with the brief history lesson behind us, we can get down to the actual nuts and bolts of this chapter – decoys, and how to use the plastic geese, or whatever they're made of, most effectively. First, let's take a look at what's out there in the way of decoys, a physical description so to speak, how one differs from another and another and another, and finally, the various pros and cons associated with each. After that, it's your decision –

Silhouettes – By definition, a silhouette is a "solid outline or profile," and that, believe it or not, describes silhouette goose decoys reasonably accurately. In the beginning, goose silhouettes were simple, often consisting of little more than various goose shapes – feeding, head up (sentry), head down, sleeping, preening, honking, or any of 101 different poses – cut from lightweight plywood and painted in colors resembling the goose species of choice. Today's silhouettes, on the other hand, are crafted of super-tough plastics, and feature damn near 3-D photographic images of live geese. They look good, I'll say, as a picture should; however, they're still silhouettes…just like they were 100 years ago.

A spread of Outlaw silhouettes in a soggy Washington barley field. Seven guns killed 28 geese – a limit – and 48 ducks over this rig before noon...seriously.

Pros

1. Silhouettes, or silos, are lightweight. This means that one man can carry and put out several dozen as opposed to two dozen shells or a half-dozen full-bodies. Sometimes a lot of decoys is a good thing; sometimes not. Still, silhouettes are there if the need arises.
2. The new photo-image silhouettes look good, and often offer a dozen or more different poses. This lends itself to realism, which in turn can lead to a more natural-looking spread.
3. Flat, silhouettes are easy to store and take up little space – again, in comparison to other styles.
4. Because silhouettes are goose-shaped billboards, they make great things to hide behind. Silos are often used around a low-profile blind, goose chair, pit, or other hide, simply as additional concealment.
5. In the grand scheme of things, $100 to $125 per dozen silhouettes is still pretty inexpensive.

Cons

1. Even the best photo-image silhouettes are still two-dimensional. This means the decoys have a tendency to "disappear" when the birds get directly overhead, and then reappear once they've passed over. Yes, it happens, but the question is – Is this disappearing act significant and long-lasting enough so as to be detrimental to the effectiveness of the decoy? Some guys say yes. Some guys, like Darrel Wise of Real Geese fame (www.realgeesedecoys.com), simply roll their eyes as if to say – "Not true." One solution to this situation is to vary the direction to which the decoys are placed; that is, if the blind is the center of the clock, then some silos will face 12 o'clock, some 1:30, some 3:30, some 5 o'clock, and on and on. Such an arrangement means that decoys will always be visible to at least a portion of the flock, except perhaps to the handful *directly* overhead. NOTE – Of particular interest is Fred Zink's theory on this appearing/disappearing characteristic of silhouettes, and how this here-gone/here-gone quality can actually be beneficial. It's a must-read.
2. I realize to be correct here I must have a Number 2; however, I can't think of any other negatives. And I'm not so sure that Number 1 can actually be classified as such. Jury's out.

Shells – Hold a reciprocating saw parallel to the ground and cut a plastic goose in half from chest to tail. Assuming the half with the head is hollow, what you're now left with is in essence the shell of a goose; hence, the shell decoy. Shells are half-geese designed to be used either directly on the ground to simulate gluttonous food-rich

My Pop inside a spread of cardboard cut-outs. As you can see, they worked just fine.

feeding birds, or in conjunction with some type of stake. These stakes serve two purposes – one, to get the decoy off the ground to where passing birds can more easily see them, and two, and in the case of such things as Avery's *Universal Motion Stake*, to allow the decoy some degree of eye-catching, realistic movement. Today's shells come in two versions – removable head, and one-piece. I'm a two-piece guy myself; however, there are lots of folks who enjoy the convenience of the one-piece, No More Headless Bodies shells. Your choice.

Pros

1. Like silhouettes, shells are typically lightweight, easily carried, quickly set, and, because they stack one inside the other, conveniently stored.
2. At roughly $80 per dozen, shells are affordable, particularly for the newcomer to the sport or the guy on a budget.
3. Was a time when shells looked…well, like geese with cosmetic problems. Today, though, companies like Avery Outdoors are spending more time and money getting their shells to look like the real thing.
4. Shells sans stakes – that is, geese sitting on the ground feeding – look like geese that have hit paydirt in terms of food, and to incoming birds, there's nothing more attractive than thinking they're flying into the heart of an All-You-Can-Eat buffet. For this reason, a lot of guys, and Fred Zink is one of them, increase the number of stakeless shells they use in a spread as the season progresses. And especially when the weather turns cold.

Cons

1. Unless you're going with the one-piece style shell, you're going to lose heads…period. There's no way around this. It's going to happen.
2. In tall stubble, especially corn stubble, stakeless shells can be difficult for far-off birds to see. Shells, in my opinion, work best in short cover, or if in taller stuff, when used in conjunction with a higher-profile decoy such as a full-body or silhouette.

Full-bodies – Just as the name implies, full-bodies are three-dimensional – full-bodied – decoys that approximate a real goose in size, shape, color, appearance, body posture…everything but the honk. Like both silhouettes and shells, full-bodied goose decoys have gone through multitudinous changes over the past several years to where today, it's often difficult to tell what's plastic and what's Mother Nature. Again like shells, full-bodies come in a couple different varieties: the popular hard, rigid body, and a collapsible or flexible format.

Traditional shell decoys like these from Avery are often used with moveable or flexible stakes so as to impart movement. It's a good idea.

Pros

1. Realism, realism, realism! Short of using stuffers (mounted or taxidermy decoys) or illegally staking a captive flock of Canadas around the pit, there's not much that can beat a full-bodied decoy for realism. You get into something like Aero Outdoors' DropZones, Hardcores, Flambeau's Judge, or the legendary Bigfeet, and I can guarantee that you'll be doing less hunting and more – much more – watching to make sure your hunting buddies aren't ground-swatting your new blocks.

2. In keeping with this realism theory, full-bodies offer a much larger array of body positions – natural body positions – than do most if not all of the other styles of decoy. Photographic silhouettes come close; however, it's a case of two-dimensional versus three-dimensional, and you see where I'm going with this.

3. With full-bodies, it's often possible to use a much smaller spread and still have all the drawing power of a 12-dozen decoy rig. In fact, and as guys like Zink will tell you, it's sometimes best to seriously downsize your full-body spread when you're hunting educated birds. Often, three or four are all you'll need. And that's better than humping 125 plastic geese into the field, now isn't it?

Cons

1. If silhouettes and shells are the F-150s of the decoy world, then full-bodies are the Cadillac SUV in terms of price. Yes, they're expensive – average is $20 to $40 PER DECOY – but when you want the real thing, you should expect to pay a real price. But consider the work that goes into creating a full-bodied decoy; the prep, the plastic, and the finishing, not to mention individually hand-painting each and every one. AND, when you consider that one dozen Hardcores ($480) will often do the work of 3 dozen high-quality silhouettes ($455)…well then, start saving your pennies.

2. Full-bodies take up space. In most cases, the guys that use full-bodies will haul them around in small trailers – a necessity when storing, transporting, and field rigging two dozen or more of the bulky things. You're going to be hard-pressed, if not nudging the impossible, to backpack a dozen Elites or Hardcores into the field. And then where to put them in the off-season. Things to be considered.

3. Although rugged, full-bodies, especially some of the higher-priced airbrushed decoys, require a little better handling than simply being thrown in the back of the truck. Jordan Bowell of Aero Outdoors talks about each Elite going into the

Shells, particularly the *h-u-g-e* ones, can double as blinds. You can hardly see the dog in this photo.

same heavy plastic bag it came in originally at the close of each hunt, and then each goose-bag being stored in a truck or trailer so as not to rub against its neighbor. That's a whole lot different than slamming two dozen shells, plus heads, in a decoy bag and heaving the whole thing in the rig.

Floaters – A full-body and a shell decoy develop a romantic interest. One thing leads to another, and BAM! – a floater. Interesting story, perhaps, but the bottom line is that floaters, or floating goose decoys, are nothing more than half-full-bodies or closed-keel shells designed to be used on the water. The Canada goose version of a duck decoy. Surprisingly, folks seem to forget that geese are indeed waterfowl, and though much of the attention today is placed on field-hunting tactics, some very memorable hunts can be had gunning Canadas, snows, and specks over water. Thus, the need for a decoy that would float.

Pros

1. Versatility. While the locals continue to pound the same wised-up birds on the area cropground, you're taking your two dozen floaters to a sandbar in the river or a backbay on a nearby impoundment, killing your limit, and getting home before they're waved a flag at the 101st flock to ignore them that evening. Floaters just

allow you to do something different. To mix it up.
2. In some cases, companies offer combination floater/shell decoys. Snap the keel off, if there's one in the first place, and you have a fine field decoy. Keel on, and you've got your floaters. One price, and two different decoys for two different hunting situations.
3. Modern floaters are much more realistic today than they were a decade ago. In other words, the static, all-upright, sentry positions have given way to mixed body postures and incredibly natural overall appearances. Half a dozen of these new-age floaters thrown at the edge of a puddle duck spread have scored more than one Canada for the guy who started out the morning specifically chasing mallards or widgeon.

Cons

1. Like full-bodies, floaters are bulky and take up quite a bit of space, particularly if they're a one-piece (non-detachable head/neck) decoy. This means logistical considerations in storage and in transportation, both to the field as well as into the field. One man can only pack so much into the field on his back.
2. I'll reach at this one as far as putting it in the *Con* side of things, but traditional – that is, non-interchangeable – keeled floaters can in most cases be

Full-bodied decoys, or simply full-bodies, have become somewhat of the norm within most goose hunting circles.

used in only one type of situation…on the water. For the hunter watching his wallet, this might be a serious consideration and might prompt a closer look at one of the floater/shell combos; however, for the man who's doing his fair share of water hunting, then there's not a problem.

Stuffers – Stuffers are literally mounted, or stuffed as some folks call it, taxidermy geese that are taken into the field and used in place of their plastic full-bodied counterparts. I said it earlier, but it's appropriate to say it again here. Short of using live geese, a tactic that while undeniably effective can result in a none-too-cordial visit from the local conservation officer, stuffers are probably the deadliest tool a goose hunter can use.

Ben Holten, who runs North Flight Waterfowl out of Richland, Washington (www.northflightwaterfowl.com), has been hunting over stuffers for the past five years. Currently, Holten guns over a spread of 120 self-mounted Canadas – or as he says, "three trailers worth." Knowing that, I figured he'd be a good one to ask about the pros and cons associated with using these oh-so-realistic, but not without their problems decoys.

Pros

1. "Guys like hunting over them. They're a big selling point for our clients," said Holten, who continued by comparing hunting over stuffers to fly-

anglers who attach their own creations to the end of their leader. "There's stories behind most if not all of the decoys," he said. "And kids absolutely love hunting over them. They think they're really neat."

2. "When you use stuffers, you have a lot of confidence in your decoy," he explained. "I mean you put those out there, those are real geese out there. They really do make a difference."

3. As with the new generation of full-bodied decoys, folks hunting over stuffers are often able to downsize their decoy spread and still be effective. "I'd take six stuffers over 100 Bigfoots any day," said Holten. "At least out here."

Cons

1. Understandable due to the inherent fragile nature of these taxidermy decoys, stuffers are very time-consuming when it comes to transportation, storage, and field placement. "I have to strap every single decoy down in the trailer individually, and that takes a lot of time," said Holten. "It's difficult to do things quickly with stuffers. Maybe you need to get out of a field quick. Or maybe it's 8 o'clock and you're trying to pick up. They just take a lot of time."

2. And then there's the weather. "You can't use stuffers in the rain," he complained. I would

Full-bodies like these from Greenhead Gear allow hunters to dramatically downsize their spreads – with incredible results. That's Shawn Stahl, by the way, creator of the *Migrator* blind.

imagine the same holds true for snow, sleet, and even a good heavy frost. Oh, and although I didn't ask Holten, I would imagine that it's not in one's best interest to leave a spread of 120 stuffers out in the field overnight to hunt the next morning. A couple coyotes and a stack of stuffers probably isn't a good combination.

3. "Acquiring the skins and doing the taxidermy work in the first place is very time-consuming," Holten commented. "My first mount took probably 20 hours to complete. Now I'm down to about six hours per bird, but it's still a lot of work. And it's no fun. The birds are greasy and dirty. Working in the summer with the heat and the flies laying eggs on the skins you're fleshing. It just sucks." But he wasn't done yet. "Girls don't like the process much either," he continued. "I boil the heads to get the meat off, and then I'm drying them in the microwave in the house. You have to do it pretty quick 'cause the skin on the heads is thin and dries out pretty fast. My last girlfriend – NOTE: Notice the use of the past tense here – told me that 'if we get married, you're never doing that in our house.' So there's that.

4. Finally, the maintenance. "Bugs and mice can wreck havoc on a spread of stuffers," said Holten. "I had a friend in Boise who went into his shed where he stored his stuffers, and there

were feathers everywhere. The mice and bugs just totally ruined them." In addition, there's the upkeep above and beyond what you'd have with plastics – mending broken legs, necks, and bills; soothing ruffled feathers; replacing, repairing, and painting bases; reinstalling eyes; and so on. Yes, they're realistic. And, yes, they work incredibly well; however, they're a lot of work.

Electric geese and other things

Wouldn't you know it. The electric duck, aka Robo-Duck, Wonder Duck, MOJO Mallard, or as it's known by any of 101 different brand names, comes onto the scene, and someone was bound to come up with a goose version of the same thing. They did. The folks at Mojo Decoys (www.MojoMallard.com) have one of the spinning wing goose decoys. There's also something called The Turbojet Decoy, which offers hunters their choice of either a speckle-belly, snow, or Canada floater that features a battery-powered prop motor. This avian outboard runs in circles somewhat like a one-armed swimmer, and that motion is supposed to convince wary birds that everything down below, save for the goose with the aquatic issues, is hunky-dory. Personally, I haven't used the goose spinner enough to come to a scientific conclusion; however, Tommy Akin of White River Sales and Marketing has.

"The best thing about the Mojo Goose Decoy," says Akin, "is that it has a remote control switch so you can turn it off and on. I leave it on when the birds are a long way off. As they get closer, I turn it on and off in short spurts. When they get within about 100 yards, I'll turn it off and leave it off until I shoot. Or, if they leave, I'll turn it back on. It's not different from the Mojo Duck," he continued. "Sometimes it works miracles, and other times it doesn't."

So there it is, experimentation at its finest. The upside to electric geese, at least as I see it, is that they do provide another tool for the goose hunter. Something that can, if all the conditions are right, work. On the other hand, these mechanical birds aren't inexpensive, costing $180 to $230, depending on the version you choose. Compared to $25 for one of Randy Bartz' *Lander* goose flags – You'll read about The Flagman here in a bit – and for us frugal folks, the choice becomes pretty clear; still, it's your call.

Motion in a goose spread is important, yet short of employing some sort of mechanical device, it's usually difficult to impart any type of movement or motion to a decoy spread. This is especially true if you're using shells. Shells lack the true-to-the-eye look of the full-bodies, and they don't provide the strobe-like appear/disappear effect that you get with silhouettes; however, that doesn't mean it's time to throw them out, thanks to a simple invention known as a stake. When it comes to shell decoys, stakes aren't an original concept. For the most part, decoy companies have always included some type of stake – often little more than a round metal stick – designed primarily to elevate the shell, thus making it look more natural. That's great, but it did little as far as motion was concerned. In 2002, however, the folks at Avery Outdoors revamped the traditional shell stake by adding a couple washers and a steel spring, and in doing so provided shell users with a platform that not only elevated the shell, but allowed the decoy to bob and weave in even the slightest breeze. Skewered as such with this new stake, the shells could rotate through 360 degrees. Translation – They changed themselves to always face into the wind, thus eliminating the need for you to get out of the your hole and move six dozen shells when your first-light northwest wind turns and comes out of the east.

Flocking. I was initially familiar with the term only because my Mother, quite the decorator at Christmas time, used to spray flocking on the Christmas tree. Flocking, as it turned out, was essentially snow in a can, and the process, I will admit, made the tree look as though it had been on the receiving end of an inch-deep fall. By definition, flocking are tiny fibers of a soft material, often wool, cotton, or something similar, that are applied to a smooth surface in order to given that surface a textured, almost velvety feel or look.

Okay, and this has *what* to do with goose decoys?

Realistic and effective, yes, but full-bodies certainly do take up the space.

Well, it seems somebody hit on the idea of using a black flocking material on the head and neck of Canada goose decoys in order to, per the definition, give them a softer, velvet-like appearance. In essence, a more natural look. And you know what? It looks damn good! Basically, the process, though time-consuming, is no more involved than scuffing up the decoys and applying the material. Today, several companies make and sell the flocking; however, from what I've read and been told, some stuff sticks and some stuff doesn't. That said, it might make sense to do a little Internet research on sites such as www.goosebusterboys.com or www.aerooutdoors.com, both of whom have flocking kits for sale. And you can always call and ask before buying. The bottom line – Does it make a difference in the field? Let me put it this way. It can't hurt, and it certainly does look good.

The last types of decoys we'll look at are what I'll call rags, windsocks, *Magnets*, and, for lack of a better term, folders. Popular among the nation's snow goose hunters, rags are just that – rags. Actually, modern snow goose rags, descendants I'm sure of the once-favored diapers or paper plate decoys, have been made to look a little bit more like a snow goose, black wingtips and all, than a mere hunk of white paper lying on the ground. Because they're lightweight, inexpensive, easy to deploy, AND compressible to the point of being able to get 1,548 in a Wonder Bread bag, white goose hunters love 'em. In most cases, stakes, either hardwood dowels or short lengths of solid fiberglass, are

Modern goose floaters have changed from the cartoon characters of old to life-life works of true art.

used to anchor the rags; however, in these modern times, headstakes – stakes with the head and neck of a goose atop – are also available for those looking to liven up their rag spread a bit. In addition to white geese, rags are also available in blue, speckle-belly, and Canada styles.

Windsocks are a sort of improved rag decoy. Socks look quite similar in appearance to rags, and operate under the same basic principle, with one major difference. An opening in the front or chest area of the decoy – an air scoop, if you will – fills the sock, thus turning it into a lightweight yet 3-dimensional and very animated representation of a goose. Unlike rags, headstakes are the norm where windsocks are concerned. The downside to socks? Well, they'll certainly work without wind, at which point they can honestly be called fancy rags; however, you need a wind in order for socks to come into their own. Windsocks are currently available in both Canada and snow styles. If you're looking to increase the size of your spread, especially if you're hunting snows, while at the same time wanting a lot of motion <u>and</u> a reprieve for your wallet, then windsocks might just be the way to go.

The Goose Magnet by Expedite International (www.trumotion.com) is what I'll call a flying decoy; that is, it's the head and upper chest of a goose, neck outstretched as if in flight, to which a pair of lightweight "wings" have been attached. The whole contraption, or as is often the case, contraption-S, is then mounted on a pole and the pole, with flying goose, erected at the edge of a

decoy spread. The idea or the illusion here is to give the appearance of one or more geese coming in to land with a flock already on the ground. Lightweight as they are, the wings of this flying decoy will flap or move with the slightest breeze, thus providing eye-catching motion where there naturally should be eye-catching motion. Snow goose hunters, at least those I've seen in southwest Iowa in the spring, wouldn't be caught dead without their Goose Magnets. Canada hunters, on the other hand, seem to be split – some do, some don't. As is the case with most of the outdoor products we hunters are subjected to, magnets are a call for experimentation.

And finally, folders. I'm going to refer to those decoys made by such folks as Last Look Decoys (www.last-lookdecoy.com) or the FUD – Fold-up Decoy…get it? – by Blackwater Decoys (www.blackwaterdecoys.com) as folders simply because they need a category all their own. Folding decoys do just as their name implies. FUDs fold flat, making for easy storage and transportation, while Last Looks can be carried either unfurled and flat, or nestled one inside another like a stack of Styrofoam cups. A couple quick twists and turns, and the decoys are ready for action. To my way of thinking, folders are tailor-made for two primary uses – one, for those folks who want add volume to their goose spreads without spending a ton of money. And two, for the freelance goose hunter, the guy who walks into a set-up and needs a decoy that looks good, yet is lightweight and easy to carry into the field. As

Taxidermy decoys, aka stuffers, provide the ultimate in realism; however, there's a lot of work involved in first obtaining the subjects, and then readying and maintaining them.

for effectiveness – No, I can't imagine folders ever replacing full-bodies or quality shells in terms of realism or out-and-out draw, but can you kill geese over them when the situation's right? Without a doubt.

Decoying Canadas: True or false

It's still a mystery to many, this arranging of plastic Canada geese with the intent of attracting real Canada geese to within, say, 45 yards. How many plastic geese do I arrange? One man tells me 10, while another says no fewer than 110. How, then, do I arrange my plastic geese? Again, Man #1, a proponent of the Random Placement Theory, suggests that it really doesn't matter. What does matter, he says, is that they're all out there. Meanwhile, Man #2 is busy drawing oh-so-detailed diagrams, complete with X-marks-the-spot – those would be the blinds, I'm guessing – and notes explaining what type of decoy goes where. Oh, and why it goes there. Finally, there's the question of where, where do I set my plastic geese in relation to such variables as blind placement, sun, and wind direction? Man #1 voices his opinions, at which point Man #2 suggests that Man #1 is a moron…and the fight is on. I get out of the way, unharmed, but none the wiser when it comes to the ABCs of arranging my plastic Canada geese.

Fred Zink, on the other hand, knows how to arrange

his plastic Canada geese. And while Zink, 33 and an Ohio boy just like myself, won't go so far as to say that decoy placement for Canadas is an exact science, there is, he'll be quick to tell you, nonetheless an art to it. None of this throwing 'em out there just to say he has them on the ground for Zink. No, sir. But then again, I wouldn't expect anything less from a guy with an outdoor resume' that includes wins at such prestigious goose calling events as the 1998 Remington International and the 1999 Avery Invitational. Today, and with much of his contest calling behind him, Zink, who also sits on the Mossy Oak Pro-Staff, is in the business of designing goose hunting products for the folks at Avery Outdoors down in Memphis. On his frequent slow days – Yeah, whatever…right, Fred? – he still finds time to hand-tune a fistful of his Paralzyer SR-1 short reed calls, do a little decoy carving, and cruise the Ohio backroads looking for, watching, studying, and listening to those things that he loves so dearly – the Canada goose.

So it was with this knowledge of Zink's background in what we'll call the Scientology of the Goose Spread that I called the man, and threw at him what just might be the nation's first true or false test dealing specifically with the hows, whens, wheres, and whys of successfully decoying Canada geese. I think you'll agree that a goodly number of Zink's answers don't only debunk many of the myths goose hunters have about decoying Canadas, but beat the hell out them, too. And so with that, Class, grab your pen-

A set of windsocks waddles in the wind not far from the shores of Port Susan Bay in Washington state. Motion is the objective with most 'socks.

cils and open your tests. Time for True and False.

True or False – The hunter with just two or three dozen Canada decoys will never successful.

Zink – "False. (NOTE – No hesitation there.) Numbers really don't play a major role in success. It's more about your location and the education level of the birds you're hunting. When I encounter very, very educated birds, I'll use two dozen. A dozen. All the way to three or four decoys. And when I say educated birds, I'm speaking of birds that are educated to the way hunters hunt them. Most hunters will use from 40 or 50 decoys to as many as 200 or more, and those numbers are basically the norm. These birds have been educated to that fact. To those numbers."

True or False – Just go with the number of decoys you have. It really doesn't matter how many you put out.

Zink – "False. I wouldn't simply use what you have, but I'd use fewer than what you have to begin with. You should use your decoys like they're tools. And you should always change. In the beginning of the season, I'd suggest using your lesser quality decoys, simply because geese will often decoy to anything early in the season. As the education level of the birds' rises, you should raise your education level by doing things such as using your better quality decoys – your full-bodies and such – or by using more or fewer decoys. Always try to change things up throughout the season."

True or False – With that in mind, Fred, does it make sense to keep an 'ace in the hole' when it comes to decoys? Or is that taking it a bit too far?

Zink – "That's totally correct. We try to start off the season using silhouettes and common shell decoys, and improve our spreads from there. Of course, it depends on your location. Where I live and hunt in Ohio, most people hunt over Big Foot decoys. Big Foots are extremely good decoys, but in my area, they don't work simply because the birds know what they are. So to answer the question, I'll not only try to hold a card back, but I'll try to find out what everyone else in the area's using and try to go a different route."

True or False – Simply mixing your decoy styles – silhouettes, shells, full-bodies – and arranging them in a haphazard manner will be just fine.

Zink – "False. I will mix decoy styles later in the season when I'm hunting flight birds or migrating birds, and you're looking for sheer numbers of decoys in the field. But on your average hunt, I don't mix decoys. When a goose comes into a spread of mixed decoys – full-bodies, shell decoys, silhouettes – they get accustomed to seeing all three types of decoys at the same time. Once they get smart to that and you pull one or two of the types of decoys, they're still smart to the remaining style. I use decoys as a tool, and I'll use one style until I see the effectiveness of that style beginning to wear off. I'll then pull that decoy and use another style, knowing that I can always use the decoy they've grown accustomed to later in the year with new geese. So I'm constantly rotating the type of decoy I'm using, and I NEVER try to use them all at the same time."

True or False – Don't mix silhouette decoys in with your full-body or shell decoys. As the geese circle, silhouettes "disappear and reappear," and leave holes your spread.

Zink – "False. The problem with a full-body spread is absolutely no movement. By mixing silhouettes completely through your spread of full-bodies and shells, that appearing and disappearing act that the silhouettes do at certain angles is the same thing that flashing wing decoys do. That flagging does. It gives the illusion of movement in the spread. That's the key to movement – appearing and disappearing. I think this example is a very good decoy tool, and I use it a lot."

True or False – An effective decoy spread for Canadas will have approximately HALF the decoys in the head-up or sentry position.

Zink – "I would say false, but this is one you could talk about for 20 minutes. It depends on the temperature at which you're hunting, weather conditions, storm fronts. As we drive along and see geese feeding in the fields, what we typically see is maybe 70 percent feeding and 20 percent what I call walkers – geese that are walking from one feeding area to another. These geese have an upright head,

Now's NOT the time to be wondering – Did I put this spread together right? You'll find out in a minute, believe me.

with a slight curve to it. The other 10 percent I call lookers, and they stay very, very still. These birds have a very high chest and head, and they're essentially looking for danger. They're not alert and they're not scared; they're just looking out for the safety of the flock. Now, as you watch geese in the air come to geese on the ground, you'll notice as the airborne geese get closer, the birds on the ground will actually begin to pick their heads up. You'll have more sentry heads among those birds on the ground. A lot of people say that if you have a lot of sentry heads in your decoys, it makes 'em look scared or alarmed. That's 100 percent bullshit. I've watched flocks on the ground that will have 90 to 95 percent of the birds with their heads up in that sentry pose as another flock approaches. These geese with the upright heads are in a threatening pose, and they're threatening because there's food – their food – on the ground. So by having a more active looking flock with more upright heads, and in conjunction with calling, you're telling those birds in the air exactly what they want to know – Food Here."

I think it's worthwhile here to let Fred continue in regards to what he claims is an old wive's tale, that being too many sentry or upright heads in a Canada goose spread is for all intents and purposes the Kiss of Death.

"I've studied geese all my life, but over the past two years, I've done nothing but technically watch, study, and photograph Canada geese feeding. And watching other geese come into those feeding flocks. I understand – not

100 percent 'cause you can always learn something new – but I have a good understanding of how wrong we are in terms of how we think about geese and how they act."

"The sentry mode," Zink says, "is a curious mode is an aggressive mode, meaning he's willing to fight over something, and that something often is food. It doesn't mean he's scared. A Canada goose in a sentry mode with a thick, puffy neck is an aggressive goose. A Canada with a very high, very thin neck, on the other hand, is very, very nervous. This thin neck, combined with silence, is a sign of danger. So look at your sentry heads. What do they look like?"

Back to True or False –

True or False – Resting, loafing, or sleeping decoys have no place in a field spread for Canadas.

Zink – "False. I believe that a field spread with shell decoys and/or full-bodies with their feet removed is more effective than any type of spread in the field. The only time Canada geese lie down to feed…two things. Number one has to do with temperature. Anything below 10 degrees, and geese will start to lay down to feed. It has to do with keeping their feet from freezing. The number two reason these geese are lying down is 'cause they've found food. Lots of food. And that's exactly what the geese in the air want to see. The most effective late-season field decoy, in my opinion, is a shell with a sleeper head on it. These

Numbers, of decoys that is, aren't necessarily the answer to all the decoy questions. Sometimes it takes 10; other times, 110 won't do it.

sleepers show that there's so much food in the field, it didn't take long for the birds to feed up, and now they're sleeping. Right there in the field. I totally believe that shells with the sleeper heads are the best late-season decoys available."

True or False – Unlike some duck spreads, there are no traditional decoy spreads – the hook, the J, the C, the V, the X – for hunting Canadas.

Zink – "I'd say that's true. In the fields, you can somewhat control the geese by showing the birds where the food is and where it isn't using decoys and decoy placement. On the water, however, geese show a tendency to always light short of the decoys and then swim in. It's not that the blind's wrong or the decoys are wrong. That's just what they do with live geese. Knowing this, one of the best water spreads is to try to create the illusion of resting geese. I'll put 80 percent of my decoys right at the edge of the bank. Close together, with shell decoys on the bank and full-bodies 'walking' into the water. Try to create a black line right at the waterline. Put the lookers (sentries) farther out and in lines swimming in, but no more than, say, 15 yards from the blind. That's about as traditional as I get."

True or False – NEVER place any of your Canada decoys outside the effective range of your shotgun.

Zink – "Never. True. I'd never place Canada goose decoys downwind of my blinds more than, say, 10 yards,

but I've stretched 'em as far as 150 yards upwind of me. Especially when you're shooting with silhouettes. Why silhouettes? The rule of thumb is that geese generally won't land among silhouettes."

Here again, I'll break away from the True or False format, and have Fred describe one of his most effective field spreads for Canadas, one that focuses on using silhouettes as the primary decoy style.

"Because Canadas won't typically land in silhouettes, you set your decoys in a long, narrow shape. Kind of like a cigar. This one's good when you have winds of 15 miles-per-hour or higher, the kind of wind where geese won't 'side-dick' you. (NOTE – I'd never heard the term *side-dick* before; however, Zink defines this maneuver as when geese approach a decoy spread from the side and don't land but merely skirt the edge out of range. Thus, I'm assuming, the *dicked* portion of the phrase). In this kind of wind, you want to keep your decoy spread very narrow 'cause decoy-wise geese will tend to slide from 10 to 15 yards from the edge of your decoys. They'll never fly over 'em. Narrow? No more than 20 yards wide, and a long line leading into the wind. You set your pit or your hunters at the bottom of the spread."

True or False – Motion really doesn't make any difference in a Canada spread.

Zink – "False. Flagging is key, and motion is key. I would say that flagging is a very good tool to get geese to come toward you, but if geese are already coming at me, I

A mixed spread of shells and silhouettes. Zink claims the two-dimensional silhouettes can provide all the motion you need.

don't flag. As far as motion is concerned, there's motion stakes that can be added to shell decoys so that they wobble. There are modified full-bodies. Windsocks. Any type of movement is important. The waddling movement like you get with the motion stakes is great."

Is it possible, I asked Zink, that if movement and motion are good things, to have too much of this good thing? Too many windsocks? Too many waddling decoys?

"I don't think so," said Zink. "Last year (2002-2003), I hunted over 300 motion decoys, and had tremendous success."

True or False – Wind direction in a field Canada spread as it relates to blind placement isn't nearly as important as it is in a duck spread over water.

Zink – "False. Wind direction is crucial. Knowing the night roost location is crucial. You have to know where the majority of your birds are coming from. Wind speed, too, is vital. When the wind blows from between 10 and 20 miles-per-hour (mph), you can control your geese very easily as the birds will typically set up – NOTE: Approach the decoys – from downwind. When the winds are 20 mph and higher, the birds will still set up downwind, but they'll do a better job of picking your decoy spread apart because of the way they seem to float or hang in the air as they approach the spread. It seems to take 'em a long time to get there, and here, you need to really be aware of decoy location and individual decoy realism. No wind situation,

10 mph or less, and I try to use a smaller decoy spread because, typically, the birds will just coast in from whatever direction they're coming from. With a large spread in that kind of situation, you give up the ability to pinpoint or focus your shooting spots. In other words, you can't predetermine with any consistency where those birds are going to land in that big spread. With a small spread, no problem."

I'm going to break from the program again, and let Fred discuss a tried-and-true Canada spread for those tough, no-or-low wind days.

"The first thing I'd try to do under these conditions is try and find a field that has a little more ground cover than normal. I'd set my lay-down blinds close together and do a very, very good job of camouflaging them. I'd call at the birds at a distance, but as they approached, I get quiet. Decoy numbers? The fewest I think I can get away with, depending on the subspecies of Canada." TIP – Fewer for big Canadas; more for the smaller subspecies like cacklers, Hutchinson's, and lessers. "I'd set the decoys out in front of my blinds about 10 to 15 yards. Maybe to one side or the other, depending on where I think they're going to come from. When the birds get close enough to the spread to tell that the calling *isn't* coming from the spread, I shut up. We call it Nobody's Home. We just allow the geese to come in on their own and light just shy of the decoys. That's the technique I use a lot of the time. I have a rig consisting of 14 stuffers – NOTE: Formerly live Canada

A spread of silhouettes in an early chopped Iowa cornfield that brought back-to-back limits for four shooters. Guess it worked.

Another mixed spread of shells and silhouettes. Sometimes mixing things up works wonders.

Avery's Travis Mueller working a flag on a flock of eastern Iowa Canadas during a November hunt. Movement in the spread, to many, is the key to success.

geese, now mounted and placed on a rugged base. Many consider stuffers the ultimate in realism – and when I use them, I'll set them up just like I explained. And when the birds lock up, they'll never quit. It's very, very effective."

True or False – Setting Canada decoys in small, widely-spaced family groups is ALWAYS a safe bet.

Zink – "False. Setting Canada decoys in small family groups in warm-weather conditions is a good thing to do; however, as the weather changes and feeding goes from a want to a need, geese don't tend to feed in small family groups. They tend to mass-feed, especially in cornfields. Anytime it's grain that might be in certain spots of a field, the birds tend to flock up more. A good rule of thumb is – The colder it is, the closer you set your decoys; the warmer it is, the looser you set your decoys."

True or False – It doesn't matter where you set your blind or blinds in relation to your decoy spread as long as you're close to the decoys somewhere.

Zink – "False. You need to know where the geese are coming from, and wind direction. You also need to set your decoys so you can somewhat control where the geese are going to land. Remember to take into consideration the sun. Where's the sun going to be when you start hunting. If possible, you try to have the birds looking into the sun in terms of your blind location. If that's not possible, then you try to have the sun directly on the blinds so that

any shadows from the blinds are eliminated. Take your time when you position your blind. Having your blind in the right spot will not only give you better shooting opportunities, but will actually determine whether or not the geese will finish to your decoys."

True or False – It doesn't matter if your decoys are a little muddy or a little scuffed up. The geese aren't going to get close enough to see those type of details anyway.

Zink – "False. You should always clean your decoys, and be using clean decoys with no mud or dirt on them. NEVER use soap. Just a scrub brush and water." NOTE – Curious, I asked why no soap. "Soap has UV-brighteners. When you apply that to your decoys, you're killing yourself. Ultraviolet light really works on the effectiveness of a decoy, especially under certain light conditions. Cloudy days are very difficult days to fool geese. Bright days are much easier to get the geese really, really close."

The magic known as flagging

Known across the country as The Flagman, Minnesotan Randy Bartz doesn't look his 64 years; however, once Bartz starts talking about geese and goose hunting, it quickly becomes all-too-apparent that the gentleman has spent the better portion of those 64 years amongst plastic geese trying to convince real geese to drop

Dave Fountain flagged this herd in from over 500 yards, but they slid off just before reaching effective shotgunning range. Here, Fountain walks out to have a discussion with the lead heifer.

Says Bartz, there is a right way to flag and a more commonly seen *incorrect* way to flag. It makes sense to do it right.

in. Understand? How Bartz has done this, and with a consistency matched until recently by few and those I'll risk calling his 'students,' has been by simply breathing life into his Canada goose spreads with a little cloth, a little stick, and a whole hell of a lot of know-how.

What Bartz has done, or rather, what he does and does so well, is known in the vernacular as *flagging*. Named after the very simple piece of equipment that serves as the centerpiece for this tactic – the flag – flagging is in its most elemental form the act of shaking or waving – *jigging*, as Bartz calls it – a goose-shaped chunk of material, usually black cloth, in an attempt to mimic the wing-flapping that geese do either while they're on the ground or as they're landing. For the most part, flagging is an attention getter; a non-auditory version of the Hail Call. It's meant, most will tell you, to catch the eye of a far-off flock of birds, with the intent being that the flag will draw them near enough that the decoys and the calls can then take over to complete the illusion. Once that happens, the flagging is done.

Or is it? Truth is, there's a little bit more to this flagging thing than merely shaking a black rag around over your head. There is, Bartz will tell you, a definite art to the act – a fact that becomes relatively clear once you take a look at The Flagman's answers to these flagging questions.

M.D. – What *is* the proper flagging technique?

Bartz – "Instead of waving the flag around in a figure-8 pattern," says Bartz, "you learn to jig it and make it look like a wingbeat. That's the way they were designed. That's the first thing…whoever's learning the technique should attempt to wrist jig the flag instead of waving the thing around like a golf swing or a baseball bat swing.

M.D. – A short flag, one of the original T-flags let's say, versus one of the newer pole kits. Does height above the ground make a difference, Randy, or are you trying to create two different illusions here?

Bartz – "The advantage to the pole is that with the pole, you're giving the illusion of a landing or descending bird instead of a bird that's already on the ground. Plus, the poles do give you the added height – I have some now that are 18 feet long – to where I can use two or three poles and give the appearance of a small family group landing in the decoys. If your birds have reached the point to where movement on the ground – a flag – is more commonplace, getting that flag elevated then is a new look to them and it becomes more convincing."

M.D. – Do you find situations where more than one flag is more effective than just a single unit?

Bartz – "Oh, yeah. Absolutely. Normally I use one flag on the upwind side, and I try to get the birds to come over the firing line. But one time near Fergus (Falls), I was hunting nine guys, all wearing white suits and hiding in the melting snow. We were on the 'X' as far as the feeding field, but the birds were just picking the guys out. So I ran back to

Minnesota's Randy Bartz, aka The Flagman. Need I say anything more?

the truck and got six flags, a mix of Landers and T-Flags, and I gave 'em to the guys and told them – 'Don't stop flagging until you have something to shoot at.' They did that – no calling at all – and you could see the difference immediately. It's a tough situation to talk about 'cause people are going to say – 'Ah. He just wants to sell six flags instead of one.' But when you analyze that situation, when you're creating what essentially is a family group landing in the decoys while all the guys around you are using just one flag, it can make a difference."

NOTE: Bartz had this to add on the subject of using multiple flags. Interesting stuff – "These multiple flags on the ground, like in the situation I just mentioned, would be a horizontal presentation. And then the two or three on the pole (pole kites) would be a vertical presentation. Combined, the two can really increase your chances."

M.D. – Is there a time to stop flagging, or do you just give the birds what they want?

Bartz – "What you've got to consider is how are the guys who are flagging…how are they covered up. These birds are used to seeing those wings, and are often used to landing right behind those birds that are landing. So if you put the flag down when the birds are 60-70 yards away and you go for your gun. I mean, you've got them looking at those wings and that's kind of their (landing) target, and then all of a sudden, you quit…It's kind of the same as calling. People say that you don't stop calling at 70 yards 'cause then the birds think something's wrong. Well, the

Pole kites, like the one being jigged by Allan Stanley here, offer a high vertical presentation to distant birds. This, says Bartz, is very visible and very eye-catching.

Flags can also be effective on snows; however, it's often suggested that multiple flags be used to simulate multiple birds when working snows.

same thing applies many times when you're flagging. And, too. Maybe you've got a guy out there with no face mask and he's hiding behind his flag. He flops that thing down, and now his bare face is shining out there like a bare ass. That's as obvious to a bird as if you got down on Main Street and dropped your drawers. I think there are a lot of people who aren't taking full advantage of the flags by quitting too soon."

M.D. – The birds are coming, coming, coming, and then slide off. The callers start pleading and laying the comeback calls on thick. Are the flaggers done until the birds turn, or what?

Bartz –"It's just like calling on the corners. A lot of times what you can do is fold the flag up and just use half of it. Just give it a kind of *wing twitch* like they'll do every once in a while. Just a real subtle movement just to convince them that there's still a bird down there stretching his wings. You don't have to be as bold as you were when you were trying to get 'em in the first time. A lot of guys around here will flag the birds on the corners. If they have the flag laying on the ground, they'll simply twist it so that one side comes up. Maybe do it two or three times, and often it's enough to get those birds to hook around and come at you again."

M.D. – It's tough to tell a man who just spent $150 on a goose call to leave the damn thing hanging around his neck, but are there times when it's better to flag and NOT to call?

Bartz – "The timely use of both – calls and flags – especially in the late season…well, I'll never go on record as saying a call isn't effective. I think that what you need to do, flags and calls, is to try to communicate with the flock as opposed to trying to overwhelm them with a contest routine. There's a lot of good callers out there who can do well in contests, but I think the birds have started to key in on that (type of calling). Now the guy who can quiet down and listen, and respond to or duplicate what's being sent to him by that flock, he's going to have the edge."

Bartz ended with these words regarding the use of ALL of the tools presently at the goose hunter's disposal –

"There are excellent callers out there who will tell you that if they had to leave one thing at home – the flag or the call – they might leave the call at home. That's certainly flattering to the flag, but I maintain that it's just like a carpenter. He wouldn't go to the job with just a saw and not a square if he was going to be building a house. A saw and a square to the carpenter is just like a call and a flag to the goose hunter."

6

The things we remember

An old man once told me – "Son," he said.
"Some of the most precious things you'll ever take
from the field have neither feathers nor fur."

As a young hunter, with blood in my eye but not yet on my hands, I didn't understand what the old man meant. Today, a lot older and a little bit wiser, the old man's words bring a knowing smile to my face. I realize now that what this thousand-field veteran spoke of were the memories – those indelible images burned into our minds by the things that we as hunters have seen and touched and felt.

Geese, magnificent nomads that they are, come and go. Riding the winds, they are invisible at times; save for the echoing cries they leave with their passing. But memories like those fostered by the photographs here are ours to keep. As are the friendships and the bonds, the likes of which can only be spawned and nurtured in the Good Lord's great outdoors.

Looking back, I think the old man had something else in mind. I think he was telling me, and in so doing telling us, that it is our duty to pass these most wonderful torches along to the next generation who will some day turn eyes skyward and search for the source of the sound.

And they, too, will smile.
I know the Old Man does.

7

Speaking the language

A goose hunter without a goose call is like a fisherman without a fish pole. What's he to do with himself?

The goose caller's vernacular

Like any other wild animal, including we humans, wild geese have a language all their own. At the risk of personifying the birds, I'm pretty safe when I say that nothing is said *in goose* that the geese themselves don't have a word for and an understanding of.

But there's more to this goose-calling thing than simply knowing what the geese are saying. Oh, no. It's not that easy, for you see, goose callers have their own vocab-

ulary. A little-known dialect, if you will. As you'll see, some of the terms – volume, for example – are relatively self-explanatory, and in fact are used in everyday speech. Others, like the mysterious *spit note* aren't nearly as well known. Okay, so maybe I could have come up with my own definition of spit note, that being any sound even remotely resembling a goose that issues forth from the call currently in my hands...often accompanied by ridiculous quantities of spit, which is then immediately followed by raucous cursing. However, that's all another issue not to be addressed here.

But back to vocabulary. To some the art of goose calling still lies within the realm of the unknown. The unexplored. And the largely undiscovered. To this end, I thought it might be helpful for some of you fledgling callers to have an English-to-Goose dictionary. A goose caller's glossary, so to speak.

Thus armed with the glossary idea, I went to Michigan's Shawn Stahl for help. As patient as he is talented and knowledgeable, Stahl, 33, whose competitive calling résumé' includes Top Five wins in 56 of his last 60 contests, as well as the 2000 World Championship and the 2002 World Team title, provided his expertise in what I found to be an easy-to-understand format. And so the educational journey began. Bit by bit, other talented young men contributed their terms and phrases, as well as their definitions, until we arrived at the goose hunter's equivalent of "How to totally remodel your kitchen in three easy steps." I'm certain there are other terms, words left untouched here; however, this should be more than enough to keep most callers busy during the off-season. And with that –

Back pressure – Back pressure as it relates to goose calls pertains more to flute calls and short reed calls than it does resonant cavity calls. It's just what the name says – back pressure. You place your hands over the end of the call and you create a constriction. You're forcing air into the call, and you're constricting it at the end – the exhaust port – with your hands. What this does is it forces or pushes air back the other way against the air you're presenting into the call. This actually makes the reed lighter and stand up better.

Shawn's Note – Goose callers will use back pressure in conjunction with forward air pressure. The more back pressure you use and the more you constrict your hands, the less forward air pressure you have to push into the call to make the call break over from the high note to the low note. The opposite is the less back pressure you use, the more air you have to present into the call in order to get the reed to vibrate and the note to break over the way it should.

Tongue position – The position of your tongue – curved or natural/straight – in your mouth during a calling sequence.

Hand position – Relates to how you physically hold the goose call.

Flute call – Generally longer, with a short mouthpiece and a long exhaust barrel.

Short-reed call – Shorter in length than a flute call, with – as the name implies – a shorter reed. The mouthpiece on a short-reed call is typically a little bit longer than on a flute call. NOTE – The reeds, says Shawn, are not physically shorter in a short-reed call as compared to a flute call. They simply sit farther back on the tone board and thus farther into the body of the call, resulting in a lesser amount of reed visible.

Craig McDonald, here at the 2003 Avery International, demonstrates the calling technique, including hand position, that helped him win the Canadian World Goose championship in 1998, 1999, and 2001.

Olt A-50 – The standard. Most of the flute calls on the market today are designed after the Olt A-50.

Volume – The decibel range of a goose call.

Acrylic – A plastic material that's commonly used to make the majority of custom duck and goose calls on the market today.

Shawn's Note – "The sound output from a call is controlled by several things, and oftentimes one can trump the other. As a rule, I feel you can get just as low (pitch) on acrylic, but it can get higher in pitch, too. Basically what acrylic offers is a very stable and consistent material that won't change over the years. Or change day-to-day with the weather."

Wood – The old standby material for making goose calls.

Shawn's Note – "There are several types of wood that approach the characteristics of acrylic in durability and sound. One would be cocobola. It's very dense and hard, making it durable. It also resonates like acrylic. On the other hand, there are softer woods like Osage orange, or hedge, that are very soft, porous, and susceptible to shrinking, swelling, and cracking. All of these wood characteristics are but variables; however, by nature, they will show a tendency toward a call that has a softer sound."

Mouthpiece – The portion of the call where you place your lips or mouth in order to present the air into the call.

Shaved reed – Most goose calls use a $^{14}/_{1000}$-inch Mylar reed, and a lot of guys will shave the tops of these reeds to

Despite the current short reed craze, wooden flute calls like this Big River *Final Flight* are still popular among many of today's goose hunters.

Two of the finest competition callers in the country – Delaware's Kevin Popo (left), and the Godfather of Goose, Timmy Grounds.

change both how the call sounds and how easy the call is to actually blow.

Competition calling – A method used to display an individual's talents with a goose call.

Lanyard – A device used to hold your game calls, usually worn around the neck.

Tone channel – The tone channel is the hole or groove in the tone board. The tone channel allows air to pass between the reed and tone board. The passage of this air makes the reed vibrate, and this vibration produces the desired sounds.

Bell or flare out – The end of a duck or goose call, usually where you place your hands.

Exhaust port – The portion of the call where the air exits.

Greeting call – Typically, the greeting call is used when the geese are farthest away. Usually the volume of the greeting call corresponds to the distance the geese are from the blind. Farther away, the louder the call. You want the geese to be able to hear it, but you still want the sound to have a natural tone regardless of the distance.

Shawn's Note – "Calling geese is not about making specific sounds designed to solicit the desired response from the geese. What most people typically refer to as a greeting call and when to use it may be those sounds that the geese react to from the time they see them at 200 yards until they pull the trigger. Me, I try more to find those sounds that make the geese lock up and commit on the first pass. Whether it be clucks, moans, double clucks, power calling, cluckin' and moanin', no calling, or whatever. The bottom line is that field experience teaches you how to read the birds and what sounds will make them do what ON THAT DAY."

Comeback call – The comeback call, typically, is a fairly aggressive call, and as a rule it's used to turn geese that have already approached your decoys and have veered off, either because they've seen something they think is wrong or, if you've shot into a family group, you're trying to call the rest of the flock back around.

Cluck – The standard sound in the goose vocabulary and in the caller's toolbox. It's a honk, but it's a very short honk. It's the front edge of the low note and the back edge of the high note, both of relatively the same length. But again, it's a short note.

Double cluck – A two-sound note. It can either be a cluck-moan, or a cluck-cluck. Too, it can either be a single goose or two geese talking back and forth.

Moan – A low high note, if that's what you want to call it. It's a contented sound, and if you want, you can change the inflection on it and go from lower to higher. You can use the moan in your comeback calls as well. It's a pretty versatile note.

Laydown call – These can vary, depending on who you ask, but as rule, the laydown call is a confidence type of call. They can be murmurs and moans – little guttural sounds – with some clucks mixed in. You can also do a laydown in a little more aggressive style. Still murmurs and moans, but a little more aggressive.

Murmurs – Murmurs are the low note of the basic two-note honk. Spelled out, it's like guh-guh, or gug-gug. It's more of a confidence type sound, and in most weather conditions, isn't heard at very long distances. Goosologists say that when geese murmur, they're just giving ground talk to each other – trying to locate a mate or a family member.

Resonant cavity call – The standard goose call that most callers started out with, and often referred to as the "ha-ronk" call. Relatively limited in the sounds they can produce, but still a very functional call. Examples on the market today include an Olt Model 800, as well as a call by famed maker, Glynn Scobey, and the late Ken Martin.

Inflection – Imparting your voice along with the forward air pressure in order to get a different sound, tone, or meaning to a cluck or a moan.

Barrel – The barrel has the mouthpiece at one end, and a hole which holds the insert at the other.

File and scissors – Tools that a lot of goose callers use to adjust or alter their reeds, either by shaving or by physically cutting the reed down in size.

Air pressure – The amount of air that is presented into a call.

Pitch – 'Excited' goose sounds are generally higher in pitch, while a contented goose will often be lower in pitch. The exception to this might be some of the smaller Canada goose subspecies – Lessers, cacklers, and Hutchinson's (hutchies), for example, all of which have naturally high-pitched voices or calls; still, an excited comeback call to a flock of Lessers will be higher-pitched, while moans and murmurs for the same subspecies will sound deeper.

Shawn's Note – "Factors that affect a call's pitch, other than composition, are hand position, tuning, and forward air pressure. As a rule, a more open hand produces a higher pitch, while a closed (muffled) hand will result in a deeper sound. With tuning, the shorter reeds are typically higher in pitch and easier to blow; longer reeds are just the opposite. And in terms of forward air pressure, the harder you blow, the louder the call, while the less you blow, the softer the call."

Tuning – The art of adjusting or modifying the reed and reed assembly on a goose call.

Break or break over – The point at which a note goes from low to high.

Tone board – The part of the reed assembly that the reed and wedge sit on.

Wedge – The part of the reed assembly that "wedges" the reed against the tone board.

Diaphragmatic air – Air that is brought up or forced up from the diaphragm as opposed to regular breaths of air from the mouth.

Reading birds – The art of watching the birds and determining from the signals they give as to what sounds – if any – to make on a goose call.

Flagging – The act of using a visual aid, often a triangularly-shaped flag, to "call" or attract geese. The flag or other device simulates the flapping motion of a goose's wings.

Richie McKnight pleads with a departing flock with his version of a comeback call on a hunt in southern Illinois.

Michigan's George Lynch of *Lynch Mob Calls* works his magic fine-tuning one of his creations. Note his toolbox in the background – That's a lot of stuff.

Finesse calling – Subtle calling, often with soft (low volume) or contented sounds.

Power calling - Usually loud and aggressive calling used to *tell* geese what to do or where they should be.

Finishing – The act of bringing the geese that last little distance into gun range.

O-rings – Rubber rings on a call's insert that help hold the insert tight into the barrel. O-rings also work to prevent air leaks between the barrel and insert.

Notice the eyes. It's one thing to be able to blow a call. It's another to be able to interpret what the birds are telling you WHEN you blow the call.

The fundamentals in action as Keane Maddy blows a Big River *Long Honker* near Russell, Manitoba, Canada, during a late morning hunt.

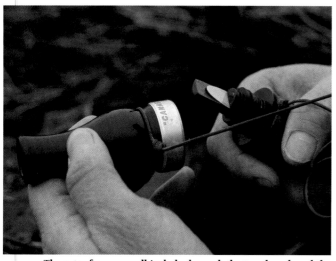

The *guts* of a goose call include the reed, the tone board, and the wedge, which holds everything from spilling out.

Aggressive calling – See *power calling*.

Guts – Often referred to as the entire assembly consisting of the reed, wedge, and tone board.

Spit note – Goose calling is getting specific with certain notes, and the spit note is one of these. Geese make what we call the *spit note*, but it has taken callers until recently to pick up on it. Today, it's fairly common in contest routines, and can be used effectively in certain field situations. As a rule, it's heard as geese are about to land;

however, it can be effective as a comeback call. Phonetically – *kuhawhoo*. It's really two notes combined, a very short *chirp* followed by a second, which sounds more like a moan.

Routine – As in a calling contest routine. Each caller is to present the same predetermined calling scenario – See the geese in the distance, turn them toward you (Hail Call), greet them (Greeting Call), begin to lay them down or land them (Laydown Call), lose the birds and call them back around (Comeback Call), and finally, land the geese into the decoys with the Laydown Call. A similar type of predetermined situation applies in duck calling competitions. The scenarios give the judges as well as the callers some guidelines to follow.

Meat calling – Sometimes referred to as "novice." Typically, the calling style in a meat calling contest is less "pretty" and polished. Routine criteria are essentially the same as in a sanctioned or open contest, but the sounds used are "nastier." Translation – The sounds used are those used to impress the birds as in a hunting situation, and not so much to impress human judges. Still, the winner is he or she who most impresses the human judges.

Team calling – Calling events that consist of teams comprised of two or three callers, the number dependent upon the specific type of event. Team calling contests are usually, though not always, connected with meat calling routines. In a team calling competition, each caller must blow a routine (See *Routine*), but must also work with his

Modern goose calls are as diverse and as varied as the people who use them.

or her teammate, paying close attention to what the other is doing. The key to team calling is to make the routine flow, and not pile notes or sounds on top of one another.

Fundamentals – The basic calling concepts and skills required for advanced work.

Reeds – In goose calls, a thin piece of material, usually made of mylar though sometimes metal, that works in conjunction with air introduced into the call to produce the desired sounds. As forward air pressure is blown into the call, the reed vibrates, and it's this vibration that creates the goose-like notes.

Cork – That piece which holds the reed down securely on the top of the tone board surface. Technically known as the wedge. While some wedges may actually be fashioned from cork, many modern pieces are made of rubber or other similar synthetics.

Insert – The business end of the call. In a goose call, that portion which holds and comprises the whole of the reed assembly, and includes the barrel and the exhaust port.

Open contest – Calling competitions which are open to any caller, regardless of age, past wins, or skill level. Callers may participate in as many Open Class contests as they wish each year.

Learning the language

Webster defines the word *learn* as "to get knowledge of or skill in (an art, trade, etc.) by study or experience."

And since he does a right good job in his definition, I'll leave it at that; however, and while it's certainly one thing to know what the word means, it's quite another when you think about the process that is learning. Rather, how do you learn to do something?

So, where am I going with this? Well, now that you have a glossary of goose calling terms as provided in large part by Shawn Stahl, as well as the nomenclature for both the inner and outer parts of a goose call, it's time to do one or both of two things. If, by chance, you don't already own a goose call, it's time to shop. Shopping, however, raises the understandable question for a large part of the nation's goose hunting population – What call to buy? And secondly, and once the type of call is determined and the purchase made, how to go about learning – There's that word! – how to make it sound like a goose. So you have shopping and you have learning. Fortunately, we've answers to both.

Answer One begins with a young man name of Kelley Powers. At the ripe old age of 25, Powers has to his credit a v-e-r-y long and impressive list of competitive calling wins, including the U.S. Open (2001 and 2003), Best of the West ('02), World Team ('02, with Shawn Stahl), the Final Approach Open ('03), and the 2003 Avery International, not to mention walking away with the World Championship in Easton, Maryland, in 1999. Not bad for a 20-year-old farm boy from Union City, Tennessee, eh? Today, Powers will proudly tell you that

Photo courtesy of Kelley Powers

Wearing what I'm assuming is a favorite rabbit-skin hat, calling champ and businessman, Kelley Powers, works his charms on a late-season flock.

Kelley Powers following his win at the 2003 Avery International in Marion, Illinois. Congratulations, Kelley. And you did a fine job there, Mrs. Powers!

he's still farming with his family, as well as playing a major role in their heavy equipment and excavating business. In his spare time – yeah, right! – he does product design for the outdoor industry, with two of his most recent and notable creations being the *Power Hunter* blind by Avery Outdoors, and the *Powers Signature Series Goose Call* manufactured by the folks at Rich-N-Tone. Combine that with an expanding radio program and an ever-growing catalog business called Final Flight, and it's easy to see that Powers has absolutely no problem staying busy. In fact,

quite the opposite is true; however, Kelley was kind enough to offer some excellent advice for folks searching for the answers to the aforementioned shopping and learning questions. And so with that, **Kelley Powers on picking a goose call –**

M.D. – There are two basic types or styles of goose calls, the flute call and the short reed. What's the difference?

Powers – In design, the flute calls are longer than the short reeds. Maybe 8 inches on average, although Sean Mann's *Eastern Shoreman* is one of the longest flutes. They produce a different sound than do the short reeds. And the reed set in a flute call is different; that is, the reed in a flute sticks out of the tone channel quite a bit more than in a short reed.

Now here's an important note, particularly for those of you looking to buy your first goose call. On this topic of the difference between a flute and short reed, Powers went on to explain that essentially, a short reed call is a cut-down version of a flute; that is, a short flute. A traditional flute call, by virtue of its length, supplies the back-pressure – See the glossary – needed to get the call or, specifically, the notes to break over – again, the glossary – on their own. The length of a flute also helps give the call, again minus the hands, some degree of tonal (pitch) variation more or less on its own. That is, you blow into the call and by varying both the amount of air AND the speed at which that air is presented into the call, you get different goose sounds – high, low, clucks, murmurs, and so on.

Conversely and lacking this barrel length, a short reed call requires that the caller create what Powers refers to as an *acoustic chamber* at the end of the call with his hands. Open hands, combined with air volume and speed, results in one sound; closed hands, plus the air variables, offer another. And in between open and closed, there's literally an infinite variety of tones and pitches available.

Okay, now what the hell does all this mean? Well, Powers explains a little further here using Tim Grounds' *Variable Tone Honker* call as an example –

Powers – "Tim makes his Variable Tone Honker that has a little insert. It has a little bell or flare-out at the end. That bell serves as your hands doing the work for you. The way it's designed, that bell creates more back-pressure to where you can simply blow into the call, and the call breaks. It's super-easy to blow. Well, you can take that bell off. When you take that bell off the Variable Tone Honker, what you have is Tim's *Guide's Best*. Now you cannot just blow into the call with your hands off the call and make the call break. You HAVE to have your hands on the call. So now you're creating the back-pressure. And now you're getting closer to the short reed style of call."

So to re-cap on this decision as to flute versus short reed call. A traditional flute call, while technically easier to use and create goose sounds, is limited in its goose vocab-

As I said, there's still a lot to be said for flute calls such as Timmy Grounds' *Variable Tone Honker* and the others pictured here.

Each – wood, polycarbonate, and acrylic – has its differences and its following. You need to find the one that's right for you.

ulary; that is, the range of sounds, particularly in tone and pitch, that it's capable of producing. A short reed, on the other hand, is technically more difficult to use, requiring hand-air-tongue-brain coordination; HOWEVER, and this is a big however, short reeds do offer you much, much more versatility and room for growth. Think of it like this. You can buy a bicycle if all you want to do is ride down to the Post Office every morning and pick up your mail. If you're happy with that <u>and</u> you're getting your mail, that's fine. That's a flute call. But, if you bought and learned to drive a 1970 Volkswagen Super Beetle to where now you could not only get your mail, but you could take that little gal down the street out for night of beer and bowling, look for a better-paying job, go fishing, AND haul all your decoys right out to the pit…well, then, that's a short reed. In the end, both vehicles/calls have their place and both can get the job done. It all depends on what sort of job you want this piece of equipment to do. Now to continue --

Materials, or rather, what the call is made of is often the next consideration. Essentially, new call buyers have three choices – wood, polycarbonates, and acrylics. In the proverbial nutshell, the difference between each of the three materials can be boiled down to price, sound, and durability. Let's take a look –

Wood – Wood is an extremely traditional material, and understandably this is one of the main reasons why folks still buy wood goose calls. It looks nice, and it lends to the call a nice, mellow tone; however, there are exotic

Short reed calls, like full-bodied decoys, have become somewhat the norm among goose hunters today; however, that's not to say that flute calls don't have their place.

hardwood calls on the market today – African Blackwood, for example – that because of their densities, sound a lot like the more modern plastic or acrylic calls. So there's that. Easy to work with and relatively high in supply, wood hits about the middle of the price scale, somewhere between polycarbonates and acrylics. Sure, prices can vary from manufacturer to manufacturer, but middle of the road is a pretty safe bet. And a pretty good price. The only downside to wood? In comparison to the other materials, wood is

Jeff Foiles, owner of Foiles' Migrators, is one of the most recognized names in the goose hunting and calling industry, and one of several top-flight choices for the new caller.

somewhat fragile in terms of being susceptible to chipping, scratches, swelling, or splitting…especially given the conditions under which goose hunters often use their calls.

Polycarbonate – A fancy name for plastic, polycarbonate calls rank high on the durability and ruggedness scale. Because they're molded and as such are easy to mass produce, polycarbonate calls are among some of the least expensive goose calls available. Too, and because polycarbonate is a harder material than is wood, these calls can often produce a louder, higher-pitched sound than can their natural counterpart.

Acrylics – With the exception, perhaps, of the wooden traditionalists, acrylic goose calls are, to many, undeniably the most attractive calls on the market; however, pretty does come with a price. Unlike the injection molded poly-carb calls, acrylics are hand-turned out of a single piece of high-density hardened resin; barrel and insert separately, of course. After turning, these calls are then hand-polished to an incredible gloss before having the gingerbread added, which can include brass bands, laser-etchings, signatures, or all of the above. You want colors? Once you've settled on the maker of your acrylic call, your most difficult decision then becomes what color. Amber, smoke, gin, red, white, blue, red-white-and-blue, black, whiskey, camouflage, ivory, ice, bourbon…it's all there.

But as I said earlier, all of this hands-on work and beauty comes with a price, as acrylics sit at the top of the money heap, often costing $150 to $200 or more. Still, thousands of these eye-catching, goose-calling machines are sold every year.

NOTE: Both flute calls and short reeds are available in all three different materials. Yes, it's traditional to think of flute calls as being of wood and short reeds of poly-carb or acrylic, and you would be correct in that general train of thought; however, there are acrylic flutes – Sean Mann's *Eastern Shoreman* – as well as wooden short reeds, Fred Zink's cocabola *Paralyzer SR-1*, for example. Again, and like the debate between flutes and short reeds, it goes back to what you want.

So with style and material behind us, I did have one final question for Powers regarding call choice.

M.D. – Does it make sense to stick with a well-known name when buying a call?

Powers – "It's track record. When I was about 10, my father gave me this little red plastic goose call. Eventually, though, I wanted something different, so I saved up my money and I went flipping back and forth through the catalogs. Back and forth through the different call makers. And I went with track record. There was this guy by the name of Tim Grounds who was doing a lot with goose calling and innovations. And him being from southern Illinois, the goose mecca at the time. So I went with track record, and I think that's a good decision today."

So track record – call it name recognition, if you want – is a definite factor to keep in mind when deciding on a goose call, whether it be your first or your 101st. Reputation, too, though perhaps similar to track record, is another consideration. How does the company treat its clients? Do they stand behind their calls? What do the folks on the Internet – www.duckhunter.net or www.flockknocker.com – think, and what have their experiences been with these various call manufacturers? One of the greatest things about the goose call business, as I see it, is the fact that, goose season aside, you can generally pick up the telephone and actually talk to Tim Grounds, Bill Saunders, Kelley Powers, Jeff Foiles, Fred Zink, and the rest of these guys – THE guys who make the calls. You and I, we can do this. And who better to talk to than guys designing, tuning, and putting their names on the calls themselves? It goes back to a very elemental statement – When in doubt, ask the man who has both the most to gain AND the most to lose.

Okay, so now we get into the meat of this particular section; that is, you have the call. Now, how do you learn to use it? For this, I went back to Kelley Powers and asked him just that –

How do I learn?

M.D. – Does it REALLY help to watch and listen to real geese? In essence, learn from them?

Powers – "Definitely, but let me back up. When someone comes to me, the first thing I explain is that what I'm saying is my opinion. What I like and dislike. When they become learned with a call, they'll develop their own opinions about what they like and dislike to use. But one thing is a constant in terms of learning – If a goose does it, it's a goosy sound; if he doesn't do it, it's not a goosy sound. And that's our encyclopedia. You wanna know the answer, you go to the field. You listen to what geese do. You find 'em in a refuge and you listen to them. Now, I can show you shortcuts. Things to do into a call to help you learn. But the actual sounds? I'm only duplicating what the real thing is doing."

M.D. – Would it help me to attend seminars and shows where the pros have booths or are giving calling demonstrations and instruction?

Powers – "It's always helpful to do something like that. Whenever I give a seminar, the first thing I say is 'Hey, nobody's an expert.' There's only one expert, and that's the bird we're hunting. I've learned a lot from guys that other guys thought were idiots. You can always learn something – little tips. Statements that the various guys make. You know, some of those things can sound bogus when you first hear 'em, but after you think about it for awhile, they begin to make sense. Most of these guys at these shows are doing this for a living, so they'll have some good general hunting tips or strategies that can be effective. But keep in mind that when they're out in the field, there's only one expert…and they're trying to fool 'im. These callers aren't the expert. The expert's still in the air."

M.D. – How do you practice?

Powers – "Most guys get infatuated with blowing…they just l-o-v-e blowing a goose call. Eventually, though, what they'll start doing is they'll form bad habits. For instance, let's say a guy has a call laying on the table and every time he walks by, he picks that call up and does five or 10 seconds on it. Nine times out of 10, every time after that, he's going to pick up the call and do the same exact five or 10 seconds. He's forming what Fred Zink refers to as a 'human rhythm.' You want to avoid human rhythms and you want to have a 'goose rhythm.' You always want a lot of variety. You want a varied goose rhythm, not a human same-same-same rhythm.

If you want to practice moans, practice moans. Don't waste your practice time doing different stuff. And don't waste your time trying to impress yourself with the stuff that you can do on a call. Don't get into that. Practice that one note. You might sound stupid doing it, but practice just that one note until you get it."

It's always good to start learning from a position of strength. Young Mr. Powers gives us just that. Use his tips and you can't go wrong.

Is it a cliché? But it does hold true – Practice Makes Perfect.

Field calling Dos & Don'ts

Those of you who have spent any time in the field, whether it be chasing geese, ducks, gobblers, or whitetails, know that any so-called list of *dos and don'ts* can not only be damn near infinite in its scope, but can also change practically from one hour to the next. They're generalizations at best, these hunting rules of the road, and we hope that they apply and as such contribute to our success. Hope, here, being the key word.

Still, and despite the fickle nature of these rules – Geese will do this, they won't do that, and you'll never see a group of birds fill-in-the-blank – there are some things in the realm of the goose caller, some *dos and don'ts* to go back to that particular phrase, that can and often do serve as a foundation for the art that is field calling. I say field calling in this instance, as I'm told contest calling has its own and very specific *dos and don'ts*, but more on that later.

Here, I go back to Mister Shawn Stahl, and take a minute to look at the calling world and its list of *dos and don'ts* through his very experienced and very talented eyes. Shawn –

1. **Don't** go to the field with a predetermined or preconceived idea of how to call to the geese on that day. Every day is going to be different. Some days they want to hear aggressive calling, and some days, they don't want to hear ANY calling.

Delaware's Allan Stanley reading and working a flock during a January hunt in southern Illinois.

Some days they want to hear finesse type calling.

2. **Do** start out with the first flock or two, and feel 'em out. I like to listen to the birds, and get a feel for the mood – if you want to call it a mood – they're in. Are they talkative? Are they quiet? And then I start out my calling according to what I've heard. And I ALWAYS try to start out with as little as possible.

3. **Don't** show your entire hand at once. I mean, don't give 'em everything you have. Save something in case the birds do something unexpected, or maybe for another day. A lot of guys will hunt the same field or the same pit and the same birds day after day after day. And if you go out and show 'em everything you got in the way of calling on Day One, what are you gonna do tomorrow? And here's something else – if the geese are coming anyway, **don't** blow your goose call.

4. **Do** try to make the birds commit to the decoys on their first approach. Sometimes you have to adjust your cadence and your tone in order to get them to do that. For instance, if I have birds 100 or 150 yards out and they look like they're going to come in high and make a second pass, I'll get a little more aggressive with some double-clucks. Some sharper notes. I'm trying to get them to set their wings that first time and come on in.

5. **Don't** call against one another in the pit. You might have three or four guys in a pit, and each one is trying to read the geese and call to them as an individual. I don't care if you have four championship callers in the pit, they don't all have to be blowing a goose call at the birds. The old adage holds true – Do as little as possible (calling) to get the birds to commit. What I like to do is pick one guy in the pit and tell him – "You're the deal today. You're going to read and react to the birds. You're the lead caller."

6. **Do** let your designated caller lead the calling AND determine the decoy spread for the morning. You know, I'll hunt geese differently than you will, and how I call will determine in part how I set a decoy spread. That's why this guy has to be responsible for not only the calling, but the spread as well. Everyone else is just going to lend background noise to his calling. Confidence sounds – you know, murmurs and clucks. Your designated caller is like the old gander talking to the flock in the air.

7. **Don't** NOT practice. I see guys leave their goose call in their glove box or in a drawer at home until the night before the season. Then they get it out and try to use it without having mastered the instrument. They haven't mastered the ability to use that tool, so they're not as effective as they could be out there.

Christian Curtis calls to an incoming bunch near Fisher Branch, Manitoba. He'll get 'em to commit on the first pass, if he can. If not, then the real work begins.

8. **Do** watch live birds year-round. You can buy instructional videos and tapes, and they're great 'cause you can listen to or watch them over and over and over again. But the best teaching tool is to watch Mother Nature and see what she does on different days. I'm fortunate that I live 15 minutes from a goose refuge that holds birds from early September through early April, and anywhere from 6,000 birds to 45,000 birds. So in 15 minutes, I can go over there and watch during different types of weather how the birds react and respond. And it does make a difference when you can get out into the field. The more days you can spend with Mother Nature, the better off you are.

Again, it's practice that makes not only for a good-sounding all-round caller, but instills the confidence you need to *become* that good-sounding field caller who consistently brings home birds.

8

Hideouts

Whether it's hunkered in a fencerow or out prone in a modern layout blind, the bottom line remains the same – You gotta hide.

et's face it. I'm not even going to pretend nor attempt to get you to pretend that every goose ever shot was done so on purpose, and out of a structure – all it a blind, hide, concealment, whatever – specifically designed for the purpose of shooting a goose. I'd like to say that, but I can't.

You see, I shot my very first goose, a northeastern Ohio Canada, while wearing a blue sweatshirt and jeans and hiding, if you could call it that, in among the still-standing stalks in roughly what would have been the middle of my grandfather's cornfield. Call it blasphemy, if you choose, but I was okay with that at the age of 15 back in 1979, and, although my philosophies about many things, goose blinds included, have changed since then, I'm still okay with that 25 years later. And during the course of those two and a half decades, I've – and I'm not bragging here, but simply making a statement – killed quite a few geese, dark and light birds both, as incidentals. Bonus birds, that is. Something excitingly extra in the midst of a duck hunt. Nothing planned but nonetheless welcome. And I think I'd be safe in saying that quite a few of you out there have done the same.

But this chapter, perhaps interestingly enough titled *Hideouts*, isn't about nostalgia or bonuses. Nor is it about a green waterfowler hunkered down in the bushes hoping that the evening flights would happen before the lightning bugs started blinking. It certainly could be, but it isn't. It's actually about the things we as waterfowlers do and the extremes we go to in order to hide ourselves from geese. It's the things we use, and those we don't, in order to go undetected by our quarry. To paraphrase Phil "The Duck Commander" Robertson – "All you gotta do," he'd say, "is be where the geese want to be, and hide." And it can be that easy. Sometimes.

To start, let's take a look at the different categories or types of blinds that are used by today's goose hunter. Just like there are shell decoys and full-bodies, silhouettes and floaters, so too are there pits, half-pits, bales, low-profile, boats, clothes…and the list goes on and on and on. So first rattle out of the box, I had to come up with a series of blind categories, several one-word tags that would serve as summaries and as indentifiers. What I came up with were **nothing**, **natural**, **holes**, and **hides**. And we'll just go from there.

Nothing

You young guys, and here I'm talking about those folks who have never legally thrown a charge of lead shot

at goose, might not remember nor even realize this, but there was a time when the only blinds goose hunters had, short of the traditional box-style blinds and those hides known simply as hunkering in the bushes, were the clothes on their backs and Old Mother Earth. Now what in the hell am I talking about?

In short, what I'm talking about is a man putting on whatever camouflage was appropriate for the situation – Can you say brown Carhartt's or Woodland pattern? – and getting flat on his back on the cold, wet, or hard ground in among his decoys. Maybe he'd pull a little corn stubble or a little bean chaff over himself. Or, if he really wanted to hide, he'd scrounge an old piece of burlap – Can you say feed sack? – and use that as an impromptu camo blanket. Snow? No problem, unless his wife or mother was looking when he pilfered one of her best bed sheets.

Was it uncomfortable? Usually. Still, these folks, and I was one of them, killed geese. Why? Because we put ourselves where the geese wanted to be, and we didn't move around until it was time to shoot at things. I mean, think about it for a minute. You lying on your back are no higher than one of today's low-profile layout blinds. In fact, and if the truth were known, a man on his back covered in a feed sack and corn stubble is actually lower; however, and as I mentioned earlier, he's also colder, wetter, and much, much more uncomfortable.

That all said, is it still possible to kill geese from a blind consisting essentially of nothing more than, well, nothing? Sure it is, just as it's possible to shoot absolutely nothing out of the finest, most well-camouflaged pit or low-profile blind ever created. The secret to success here, I believe, lies in scouting, scouting, scouting, *and* being just a little Type-A and anal retentive when it comes to naturally – Key word: Naturally – blending into your surroundings without going to the trouble or expense of a blind, per se. Speaking of which…

Au' natural

Call it a confession if you will, but I'm sure I've killed more geese while hiding in the bushes than I have from a by-definition blind. And I'm not talking about incidental gunning during the Lead Days of Yore. You know, the December rabbit hunts where you heard the geese coming a full minute before you saw them, giving you more than enough time to (1) remember you had your duck stamp in your wallet, (2) recall correctly that goose season was indeed open, and (3) drop to one knee behind a sparse clump of frost-killed goldenrod that immediately went

As long as it's up, standing corn is one of the most effective – and most traditional – goose blinds there are.

from being weeds to being blind. Ah, the good old days.

But nostalgia aside and at the risk of offending the modern purist goose hunter, there's a lot to be said about hiding in the bushes, the *bushes* hereafter known as a natural blind. Where they're available, you're going to awfully hard-pressed to do better than a natural blind in terms of concealment. Why? The geese know it's there, and they've come to accept this natural object – a fenceline, a beaver house, a briar patch, an old house foundation…all things from which I've gunned geese while either seated on, hidden in, or secreted behind – as just that, a natural object. In other words, nothing to fear. A tree line. Cattails. Standing corn. Soybeans before harvest. It really doesn't matter what the natural cover is, just as long as two criteria are met – one, the geese accept it, and two, it hides you from the geese.

Over the years, and this is a rough estimate so bear with me, I think I'd be safe in saying that 75 percent of the times I've used or I'm using natural blinds have been under pass-shooting circumstances. Now, before anyone who might jumps on the words *pass* and *shooting*, let me say that there are two primary keys to successfully pass-shooting while hunkered in the bushes. One is a current and working knowledge of the flight lines into and out of the area you're gunning. And the second, and one which unfortunately quite a few folks seem to have trouble with, is range estimation. Let me address the first here; the second, I'll talk about in the next chapter.

Here in Iowa, there's a little 150-acre marsh just 15

minutes from the house that each year holds a goodly number of Canadas, and in the spring, transient white geese. Given the right wind, that being our predominant northwest wind, these geese will leave the marsh through a break in the low willows that's perhaps 150 yards wide. Not all the geese, mind you, but enough to make hiding in the goldenrod and foxtail that covers that particular area more than worthwhile. A friend of ours has hunted this little piece of public ground since the early 1960s, and can usually count on a Canada or two, when they're around, simply by setting up his small folding chair in the middle of this traditional flight line and being somewhat choosy about what he shoots at. The bottom line in Bud's case is that it's awful hard to argue with success, especially when it's consistent success.

My point, what with the story and all, is this. If you're willing to learn an area well enough to establish the birds' regular flight line or flight lines into and out of that area, hiding au' natural, sans decoys, can be a very, very productive goose hunting method. But it's a matter of watch and learn, watch and learn. Guess, and you're likely to be disappointed.

A couple final notes on this pass-shooting from natural blinds concept –

1. Because decoys aren't involved in pass-shooting from natural blinds, you don't have the *decoy-shy* element you might with a spread of plastic geese

2. In the same vein, because there is no blind where there shouldn't be a blind, the birds aren't *blind-shy*. That said, pressured geese can and will learn, for lack of a better term, to avoid solitary clumps of cover – fence lines are a prime and well-known example – or anything capable of hiding a human predator. Better to pick a natural blind that's part of a larger collection of similar cover, when possible, than to focus on a single, potentially spotlighted hide.

3. And finally, and while some may disagree, the fact that you're shooting birds from these natural blinds, at least in theory, between feeding and roosting areas, means you're not burning them off of either; that is, a good natural blind location should last for the whole of the season. Some do, and some don't, but most should.

Earlier I said that 75 percent of those times I've use natural blinds have been in pass-shooting situations; that is, without decoys. However, there may be times when natural blinds with a decoy spread can prove more effective than those without. Take, for instance, the educated birds here in eastern Iowa. Given a season opener in late September, the Canadas 'round these parts are awful wily come 1 November, and lately, they've taken to lighting in cut soybean fields where there's absolutely no where to hide a body. Sure, pits would work, but farmers around here are somewhat hesitant to let folks dig big holes in their livelihoods. Couple that with the fact that these open-field birds are notoriously decoy-shy, and you have a situation that, in understatement, is tough.

In the fall of 2003, we hit upon the strategy of using six full-bodied decoys set 75 to 80 yards out into these open bean fields. We, on the other hand, hid ourselves in the horseweed-choked fence lines on the edge of the fields. Wind direction didn't seem to matter, as long as we positioned ourselves between where we thought the birds were roosted during the day and this mini-spread. No, we weren't shooting geese squared up and finishing above the decoys, but we were consistently killing Canadas – and a trio of uncommon, at least in eastern Iowa, speckle-bellies – that were eyeballing the decoys BUT fully prepared to slide off before ever getting close. Positioned as we were some 80 yards away, our shots were at 35 and 40 yards at hard-hunted Canadas that had no idea we were anywhere in the section. Did it work all the time? No, but it worked often enough for me to include it here.

Holes

I could go into a lengthy discussion on the history of pit blinds and geese, but why? Let it suffice to say that years and years ago, some blackpowder-shooting guy, tired of watching geese from a distance and unable to hide in a field filled with birds but devoid of cover, told his buddy over strong ale in the tavern one evening – "You know, I'm gonna dig me a hole right in the middle of that field. And I'm gonna cover it up with me in it. That'll teach those geese." And he did. And it did. And the now-common practice of hiding in a hole and shooting geese from the interior of this man-made cave was born.

Yes, there are few goose hunting hides as effective in their concealment as a pit blind. With nothing above the surface of the ground to serve as a warning, geese have no reason to hesitate. Or at least that's how it works... in theory. The truth is, pit blinds, though undeniably positive, aren't without their negatives.

Pit Blind Positives

- **Pit blinds provide excellent concealment far away from any natural cover** – As I mentioned earlier, it often doesn't take geese long to learn to avoid anything capable of concealing a human being. Because they can be located literally in the middle of nowhere, if *nowhere* is where the birds want to be, pit blinds are then advantageous from a security standpoint. That is, the blind can be located AND well hidden where the birds feel the most comfortable, therefore making factors such as decoys and calling all the more effective.

Me and Maggie crouched in the Scotch Broom alongside a Washington quarry pond. As for the hair – Remember, even Grounds had hair like that back in the day.

- **Pit blinds are typically comfortable and roomy** – Yes, I've hunted in some pits that were tight and cramped; however, most were larger than several of the apartments I lived in during the 1980s... which isn't saying much, but you get the idea.
- **Pit blinds provide much in the way of protection from the elements** – In keeping with this comfort thesis, pits are great in keeping you out of the wind, snow, sleet, rain, and whatever else might be happening outside the hole. And comfort, believe it or not, is important to success as a comfortable hunter is a guy who's going to sit all day in a pit as opposed to a couple hours crouched in a fence line or six hours in an unheated low-profile blind.
- **Pit blinds compensate for those who cannot keep still** – More than anything else, movement scares game, be it ducks, geese, deer, turkeys, whatever. Pits, then, help hide those who can't sit still.

Pit Blind Negatives

- **Pit blinds are damn hard to move in the middle of a hunt** – "I won't put a pit blind in a field until I've hunted it for a year," says Paul Sullivan, 56, and currently the owner/operator of the Washington-based *Burbank Goose Club*

Julie shares a pit blind with Allan Stanley during a hunt in southern Illinois. Pits are an excellent way to hide; however, they're not without their downfalls.

(www.burbankgoose.com). A waterfowl guide for more than 34 years, Sullivan has spent more than his fair share of time positioning, building, and hiding in pits across the eastern part of The Evergreen State. "We only hunt geese here three days a week, but I'm out there seven days a week watching birds. And I can tell you on every one of my fields where the sweet spot is. And the only thing I can tell you about a sweet spot is that it's something you gotta find yourself. I can't tell you what constitutes a sweet spot, but I can tell you what I think are some of the things that go through a goose's mind when he wants to land in a field." That said and knowing how difficult it can be to move a hole in the ground, especially on short notice, it then becomes evident that great care should be taken in determining where the pit goes **before** the digging begins. More on that later.

- **Pit blinds can be difficult to camouflage CORRECTLY** – "The biggest negative to a pit blind is that they're extremely hard to camouflage," says Sullivan. "If you're on the edge of a field, it's relatively easy to set up any kind of a blind. We have an aboveground blind that's 13 feet long and that's a big obstruction in a field, but if you set up on the edge and properly camouflage it, the geese don't mind it at all. But when you get

out in the middle of the field and you have something that looks like a big rectangle or square out there. Those geese are used to getting shot at out of things that are big and rectangular. Unless you fly over a pit situation in an airplane, it's really hard to understand that pits can stand out. And they do stand out, sometimes like a sore thumb."

The best advice I can give you when it comes to camouflaging a pit is to live by this motto – There's no such thing as camouflage that's TOO complete. Too obvious, as in too much natural cover? Yes, but not too well camouflaged. Sullivan typically spends up to 90 minutes prior to each hunt...that's every day...stapling native materials to the lids of his pits. Just sprucing them up, he'll tell you. "When we put those lids back on and people start walking around," Sullivan says, "I can guarantee that someone's going to walk back into those pits...even if they just got out of it. That's how well a pit needs to be camouflaged."

- **Pit blinds and megaphones have much in common** - "One of the biggest drawbacks to hunting out of a pit," says Sullivan, "is the fact that it acts like a big megaphone. You don't realize this until you have everyone get out of the pit, put the lids up, and have somebody in the pit talk. You cannot believe how that echoes out of the pit. And it's not the talking that bothers the geese, it's the metallic noises. Any sound that they're not used to hearing. Actually, people talking in the pit isn't that bad. I've actually had geese try to land on the pits while we're inside talking and laughing 'cause it sounds like geese gabbling. But any of the unusual sounds? You'll never see those birds again. You'll never hear those birds again. You may not even know they were there." Bottom line? Keep the noise to a minimum, voice or otherwise.

- **Pit blinds and height and visibility** – Just like American shotguns are made to fit the Universal Shooter – 26 to 28-inch fingertip to armpit, slightly under 6-feet tall, weight proportionate – so, too, are pit blinds; that is, one size fits most. But what if you're 5'2" or 6'6". Short – no pun intended – of altering the blind itself, which ain't gonna happen, the small in stature are going to stand on a bucket and the big ones are going to crouch. That's all there is to it. And as for visibility – well, let's just say I like to look around, probably to my detriment at times, and pit blinds, even those with well-constructed lids, often have a way of getting in the way in terms of being able to keep an eye on the birds as they work. Solution? This visibility issue would probably fall under the category of Necessary Evil, although I have seen pits with dome-type lids, including one that actually used spring-loaded shell decoys as lids, that allowed 360 degrees of visibility. So it varies, and that's the bottom line there.

A note or two on pit blinds before we head into the last category –

Wind currents, the elevation or topography of the land in question, obstructions around the field itself. According to Paul Sullivan, these are just three of the more major factors than can contribute to the location of any field's *Sweet Spot*; that is, that spot or spots on any given piece of ground where, for whatever reason, geese prefer to land. All fields have them, but it's up to you to find them.

"In my 130-acre field," says Sullivan, "there's two sweet spots. In my 60 to 80-acre fields, there's going to be one. Maybe two. And when you find those spots, even though the birds have finished feeding and left from a certain spot the night before, they're going to come back to a regular spot on a regular basis. And that's how you find 'em. By watching 'em. Once you find that sweet spot, you don't want to put your pit right on it, but you want to put your pit just upwind of it."

And then there's safety

"Somebody has to be in charge of the pit," says

Pits keep you well-hidden, and protect you from the elements.

Sullivan. "This means keeping people quiet. This means giving people instructions ahead of time so everyone knows what's going to happen. It entails a safety talk to everyone involved, which includes –

- Keeping the safety on all the time except when you have the gun up to shoot
- Never pointing that gun anywhere except out front where the geese are
- Not shooting geese on the ground except when given an order by a guide or pit captain
- Not shooting across anyone
- Not shooting at less than a 45-degree angle so you don't muzzle blast anybody

"I've had guys shoot right through the top of the pit," he continues. "They get excited and they take the safety off when the geese are close. Then when they go to get up, they think they're taking the safety off and they pull the trigger. I saw a guy shoot the end of his buddy's gun off by shooting to the side. There's geese to the left and there's geese to the right, and he shoots the end of his partner's gun off."

But then this should all go without saying. Be it pit, brushpile, or soggy depression in the ground, it's always – ALWAYS – safety, first and foremost. I have yet to see a Canada goose worth a man's life, and unless technology changes, it's impossible to call back 1⅜ ounces of steel BBs once they've left the muzzle. No matter how hard you try.

Photo courtesy of North Flight Waterfowl and Ben Holton

Anything that's created with a backhoe usually *isn't* all that easy to move around. Such is the case with pit blinds.

Hides

Just as soon as I make the comment that I've touched on all the different types of goose blinds, someone, and probably rightly so, will come along with a list of those I haven't mentioned. So with that said, I won't say it. What I will say, though, is that we've reached the point here where it's time to discuss, finally, those hides – Hence the subtitle, eh? – that might be considered somewhat traditional in terms of geese and goose hunting. Here, I'm going to define a *hide* as something other than a fence line or a hole, and which is designed or meant for the shooter to be concealed either in or underneath. Many categories of such blinds exist, with more it seems being introduced to the sporting public each season; however, there are a handful of these categories into which most of the blinds used today will fall, including –

Boxes – Here I'm using the word *box* to mean any type of traditional box-like structure; that is, four sides and a roof, or something that most of us would think of when speaking of your basic at-the-water's-edge duck blind. Believe it or not, and even in this most modern age, box blinds still have many applications in the goose fields. Paul Sullivan, whom you met earlier, makes his *Maximus Blind*, which is essentially a cube made of ⅝-inch steel

conduit and covered with what they call an EZ-FAB material – a diamond mesh poly-product. The material is woven with native vegetation, and the whole deal placed wherever appropriate for the day's shoot. The nice thing about blinds such as a *Maximus* and those like it is that, unlike traditional permanent boxes, these new boxes are portable, and can go where the geese go. Regardless of whether your box comes from a factory or your own workbench, the keys to success are three: Location, attention to camouflage, and location. Notice the common denominator there?

Decoys – The use of decoys as blinds is nothing new; however, with the advent of the modern layout blind – we'll get to that in a minute – the instances of folks actually hiding behind or underneath decoys has fallen somewhat by the proverbial wayside. It's unfortunate, too, because decoys can make effective hides. In some situations, they can be as effective as any hole or low-profile device…in some situations. And while there is no arguing this lapse in popularity, a magnum Canada shell on your chest and a silhouette on either side of your head is certainly a tactic worth mentioning.

Chairs – Not content, I'm assuming, with simply slapping a decoy on their chest, someone, years ago, came up with the idea of combining a camouflaged chaise lounge with a king-sized goose shell, and thus was born what's known in the field as the Goose Chair. In operation, the chairs simply allowed the gunner to recline with his or her shoulders off the ground, while the decoy served, for lack of a better word, as the blind proper. Slots cut into the decoy allowed the shooter to keep an eye on working birds. My personal experience underneath goose chairs has been minimal, and that limited to hunts in the Pacific Northwest; however, when they've worked, they've worked well, and seem particularly effective, for whatever reason, for hunting ducks. My thoughts on the matter are this – For the same money or just a bit more, you might be better off and better served in a layout blind. It's all about versatility, I think.

Bales – We all knew it was only a matter of time before someone put two and two together and came up with the now-infamous Haybale Blind. Well, they did. And they sold. And they can work. Understandably, these fake round bales work best when used in fields where there already are round bales and the geese are accustomed to seeing round bales. Don't be surprised if you throw one of these blinds into a field where there are NO bales, and the birds seem a little reluctant to come near. Those that do – well, they probably should be removed from the goose gene pool. Still, these options, and that they are, can and do have their place and their following.

Boats – An entire chapter could easily be devoted to gunning geese over water from boat blinds; however, I'm not afforded that luxury, space-wise, here. That said, let it

All pit blinds aren't created equal in terms of wall height and visibility. And being able to see is relatively important...

Hides don't have to be elaborate to be effective, as evidenced by this white bedsheet – Thanks, Ma! – and white 5-gallon buckets.

These interesting blinds were made of camouflaged metal conduit boxes, and could be very easily moved should the situation warrant.

suffice to say that the same boats and their accompanying blinds from which ducks are gunned can serve double-duty as goose blinds; that is, if there are geese about, and they choose to venture within shotgun range. Truth be known, most of the boaters I've had the pleasure of hunting with over the years, save for those specifically targeting diving ducks, have included a handful of Canada floaters in their day-in/day-out duck spread. Set off to the side in that anti-social goose-to-duck manner to which we've become accustomed, such water spreads often produce surprising results. Goose specific water spreads from boat blinds? I'm not particularly well-versed in the art, but there are those – Nebraska's Tommy Stutzman, Tony Toye from Wisconsin, and a list of gentlemen we've come to know here in the Midwest – who wouldn't have it any other way, and we'll discuss that a little more in-depth in Chapter 9.

Layouts – And finally, layout blinds. Since the early days of Ron Latschaw and his then-new Final Approach blinds, these low-profile, single-man nylon and steel tubing hides have revolutionized the way we hide from and hunt geese. Period. No more digging holes. No more lying on the cold, wet ground. And no more hiding in fencerows and watching cover-shy Canadas skirt our position at 150 yards. Nope. Now we can, as Tim Grounds says, "get down and cover up" quickly, easily, and effectively. And best of all, we can do it precisely where the birds tell us to – Right on the X!

Today, several companies, including Latschaw's Final Approach (Kolpin Outdoors), Avery, and Cabela's being just three, manufacture layout blinds, and most come in a variety of configurations and camouflage patterns. Which brings us to a question – How to choose? And that, in and of itself, leads to such inquires as why they work and how to use them in the field.

A three-time Tennessee state duck calling champion, Bill Cooksey currently serves as the public relations front-man for the Memphis-based Avery Outdoors, Inc., makers of the *Power Hunter*, *Finisher*, and *Migrator* series of layout blinds. An avid waterfowler – No, duh! – Cooksey spends more than his fair share of time hunkered in these layout style blinds, and had these things to say about their selection, use, and basic reason for existence.

M.D. – Why do they work, Bill? I've been told it's because geese have no depth perception, and therefore don't recognize the blinds as a 'rise' in the topography. Any truth to that?

Cooksey – "I don't buy the argument that geese have no depth perception. It may not be the same depth perception that we have, but then again, I've tripped over camouflaged ground blinds in a field. If they're built right and they don't have a boxy look to them, your eyes don't pick 'em up as easily. These blinds all angle down toward the ground, especially the front or front angle or where you'll typically have the birds approaching from. If you walk around a decoy spread from the back, you pick up

Ah, yes. Hiding under a decoy. Don't laugh. There's been a ton of birds killed by guys hiding underneath big plastic geese.

those blinds pretty easily 'cause of the square backs. But if you walk around from the front, you can't pick the blinds out as easily because they naturally slope up from the ground."

M.D. – Anything else?

Cooksey – "There are no shadows. Shadows are THE main enemy of the ground blind. If you have a ground blind that's throwing a bad shadow out front, you're going to have problems."

M.D. – There's several of these types of blinds on the market today. How would I go about choosing one from the many? What qualities am I looking for?

Cooksey – "A – It must be easy for someone to get to the spot that they want to hunt. That's a very important thing, and a lot of people don't think of that. If you can't get it there, it doesn't matter how good the blind is. B – It has to have a profile that eliminates shadows. And C – It has to be comfortable enough that you can sit in it without moving around a lot, and you can wait out the birds. Visibility is important in different blinds just because of the way they fit different people. To me, the Power Hunter has the best visibility and I can find birds easily out of it. But I have friends who find the Finisher or Migrator easier to find the birds out of. There, it comes down to finding one of the blinds that fits you physically."

M.D. – Okay, I have one. Now what?

Cooksey – "Practicing in the blind in the off-season would make a lot of sense. I'd recommend that. Even if

you can't shoot from it, practice sitting there with your gun. You could set up this blind in your living room in the off-season and just practice sitting up in it. If you could get one out and practice shooting clays with it, that would be great. Not only to practice getting out of the blind and sitting up to shoot, but to practice physically setting the blind up. There's a lot of people who take the blind out of the box and never set it up before going to the field the first time. Once you've done it a time or two, any of these blinds can be set up in seconds. But if the first time you're trying to do this, it's in the dark and it's 18 degrees, it's gonna take a while."

M.D. – Next?

Cooksey – The first thing you need to do after you've practiced setting up your blind and sitting up in it is to go out and mud the blind. I'm sure you're getting that from everybody. You HAVE to mud it. Take a bucket and get some dirt that's indigenous to the area. It doesn't have to match perfectly, but you need to get some dirt, mix it up with water, and just slather it all over the blind. Let it dry, and then just brush it off with a stiff broom or something like that. That's going to take that shine off. It doesn't matter what we do with camouflage, fabric is going to have a natural sheen to it. Well, get that mud on there and it's gonna take that shine off.

M.D. – Fast-forward to opening day in the field.

Cooksey: The next step is getting cover that matches your field. And if you're in a field that has very light or

Chairs, also known as goose chairs, are another option available to the hunter wishing to hide in something other than a hole or a hedgerow.

sparse cover, that's a tough thing to do. In those cases, I'd recommend a lot more mud. The guy who's going to hunt a field of winter wheat? Get a **t-h-i-c-k** layer of mud. That's one thing with a winter wheat field…you see brown spots all over the field where there was too much water or they didn't get enough lime on it or whatever. So if you mud the heck out of that blind so it's brown or just a black muddy looking thing, you'll still kill birds.

M.D. – It's me and three buddies in the field, each man with a blind. How do I want to arrange these blinds?

Cooksey: Typically, I'm going to set the blinds about three feet apart. That gives us enough room to put decoys between them. That's your main thing. If you get decoys in between the blinds, that tends to break up the line. You want your blinds close enough so you can talk. A big part of waterfowling is the social aspect. Plus, the safety factor. I want to be close enough that I can say 'Get down, guys' without having to scream.

M.D. – Blinds in a line has become the traditional layout set-up, but is there a time when you might do something different?

Cooksey: A small group of guys who were all friends and maybe used to hunting with one another, AND there was no wind. A day when the birds might come at the blinds from any angle. It might be advantageous to at least begin the day by facing the blinds in different directions. But here, remember I'm talking people who know each other…just from a safety factor.

M.D. – Is it possible to set the blinds incorrectly?

Cooksey: I guess – Answers hesitantly – that it would be possible to position one of the blinds incorrectly. My first thought when you asked that question would be that that's actually one of the strengths of the blind. You can find out quickly if it's positioned wrong. If the birds are flaring off the blind – just like any other times the birds are flaring – you can get out and look. Is it throwing a shadow that you hadn't noticed earlier 'cause you set up in the dark? Are you on the crest of a knoll instead of just behind it or just ahead of it? That could pose a problem. These are things that you might not notice or realize before you start hunting, BUT these blinds are so easy to move. When it's not working, it just takes a few seconds to move the blinds and they're working now.

Nothing ventured, nothing gained

You know. When everything was said and done, and each of the four categories had been addressed, there still were a handful of goose blinds that hadn't been discussed. Things that I'd seen or heard tell of over the years. Hell, some of them I've done myself, with, I must admit, varying results.…most of which could best be described as poor. Still, and as the name of this particular section implies, nothing ventured, nothing gained. There is no

Like short reeds and full-bodied decoys, the layout blind has, for many, become damn near a must-have item.

such thing as silly, if, that is, you think it has a chance – even an outside chance – of working. It's like I tell turkey hunters when the topic turns to oddball locator calls – things like loons and cows, guinea hens and elk bugles in Ohio – and how self-conscious they feel making all those strange noises. "Look at the way you're dressed, for God's sake," I tell them. "And consider that fact that you've gotten out of bed at 3:00 each morning for the past four weeks straight to chase…and not too well…a bird with a brain the size of a butternut. You feel silly?"

And with that, my point is – Nothing ventured, nothing gained.

Body-booting – Now the guys on the East Coast are going to think it odd that I've included the act of body-booting in this Miscellaneous category seeing that they are quite fond of the method, and, in many cases, do quite well at it. Body-booting, for those who don't know, can be condensed by way of explanation to the art of standing up to your nipples in near-freezing water behind a goose silhouette – your blind – while any number of plastic geese ride the waves around your person. A flock of Canadas approach, and you simply conceal yourself from the nipples up behind your cut-out goose. In some cases, booters will hold their shotgun; however, traditionalists, or at least I've been told, use blind-decoys that feature both a gun rack as well a small box for shells, calls, portable bilge pumps, and any number of pieces of equipment specific to the art. While I've never body-booted for geese, I have

Angled sides and a long sloping front make the new layout blinds invisible, while inside, padded backrests, leg room, and storage compartments make them awful comfortable.

Relatively lightweight and collapsible to some extent, layout blinds are easy to transport into the field and quick to set up once you're there.

Because layout blinds are so portable, they can easily be moved if the birds tell you that they need to be moved. You just have to listen and understand.

for ducks, and found it quite effective, particularly on pressured birds that have seen everything from fenceline hidey-holes to boats that look more like raffia-covered barges than they do blinds. You just never know what's going to work, and sometimes the best thing you can do is be open – very open – to suggestions.

Horse costumes and cow cut-outs – Years ago in a book on waterfowling, I ran across a series of black-and-white photographs of two guys in a two-part horse costume – Yes, I said horse costume – who decided that making the transformation from human to equine was going to be the way to sneak up on a bunch of Canadas feeding in the middle of an open field. Once, the captions read, they learned that geese are somewhat startled by the sight of a horse climbing out of a truck and over a barbed wire fence, the two gunners started to enjoy some success. They'd meander and graze and graze and meander – Hell, maybe they even dumped, no pun intended, a half dozen Hostess chocolate cupcakes out the back for realism…A terrible waste, no pun intended, of chocolate cupcakes, but when there are geese at stake, eh? – until they were within gunning range. Then they'd drop the suit and shoot their geese. Or so the story goes.

Then, just about the time you think that horse costumes have gone out of vogue with the modern goose hunter, along comes the cut-out cow. Or technically, the cow silhouette. As you might imagine, the cow silo consisted of a plywood cow – head, neck, and body – for

which the hunters, preferably two unless you're living close to a nuclear facility, provided the legs. Like the horse costume, the "cow" would mosey along until reaching effective shooting range at which point the shooting could commence. As I've been told, the cut-out cow has been used throughout the Midwest in recent years in response to the exploding snow goose population and the subsequent higher education that these birds have been receiving. Maybe it's a necessity being the mother of invention sort of thing, but hey, I'd try it.

Goose suits – I'd heard tell of this thing called the *Goose Suit*, but I'd never seen one until Randy Bartz, The Flagman, showed one several years ago at the Game Fair in Anoka, Minnesota. For those unfamiliar with the garment, the Goose Suit is just that – a retro-fitted set of coveralls colored and designed to make the wearer look like a giant bipedal Canada goose. The theory and intent behind the suit, I'm assuming, is two-fold. One, it serves as its own camouflage, actually letting the wearer become an integral part of the decoy spread. And two, the suit doubles as the world's largest goose flag. All the wearer must do is wander around, flap his arms, scratch, itch, convulse, bend, peck, waddle….anything remotely resembling something a goose might do. This motion, coupled with the general appearance of the suit, attracts geese from great distances, geese that come, I'm guessing, to stare and make generally unkind comments about "Fred the Mutant Canada" down below. Who knew geese could be

Communication between pits can be vital to the overall success of a hunt. Here, Richie McKnight again orders out for pizza.

Randy Bartz and the infamous Goose Suit. I hope he doesn't hate me for this one.

so cruel?

The VW Canada – Again with the pictures in a waterfowling book from some time in the 1970s. I want to say that the fellow was from the Rochester, Minnesota area; however, before anyone from Rochester gets all excited, let me say that what I do remember was that this particular individual lived and hunted east of the Missouri River. With that behind us, what this guy did was to take an early 1970s Volkswagen Beetle and paint it up to look like a Canada goose. The open doors were wings, and the beast even sported a large – a v-e-r-y large – Canada goose head and neck that sat, perhaps not surprisingly, on the hood. Come hunting time, the gentleman would drive the Bug into the field, set his decoys around this automotive Mother Goose, and then recline in relative comfort – VW = Comfort? – until the birds made an appearance. According to the man, his ruse worked, and worked quite well – success, I'm sure, heightened only by the fact that he would occasionally wear a goose suit while simultaneously seated in his German-made blind. Though not an expert on such things, I would imagine that the VW Canada worked on what I'll call the Sensory Overload Principle. I mean, can you see any Canada goose passing this combination by without at least a look?

The golfer – Now this one may fall under the heading of Urban Legend; however, I'm going to mention it regardless. I heard about it from an acquaintance in northern Ohio who, as the story was told, was actually there and took part. This hunt, it seems, happened during the early years of Ohio's September goose season. A group of guys had permission to hunt a local golf course where, as is often the case, a large bunch of Canadas were making a nuisance of themselves. The first couple days could best be called traditional – camouflage, decoys, dogs, dead geese…the whole 9 yards. The third morning, however, the group discovered that these once-trusting geese now realized they were being hunted, and that their original strategy of blinds and such just wasn't working. It was about this time, though, that one of the party noticed that the geese paid absolutely no attention whatsoever to the golfers, the shorts-clad, club-swinging, bag-carrying golfers. Not needing to be hit by the proverbial stick twice, the guys switched gears, trading their camos for Hawaiian print polyesters, their gun cases for club bags, and their decoys for Coleman coolers. Instantly, they were back into the thick of things, until the birds became completely people-shy, and relocated themselves to a nearby city park pond where they spent their days gorging on stale popcorn, Wonder Bread, and Cheerios. True? I don't know, but if it was true, I'm willing to bet folks really paid attention whenever one of these players yelled FORE!

9

The species and the seasons

It's sights like this that bring us out day after day, season after season.

Up 'til now, I've talked about guns, gear, geese, decoys, blinds, calls, calling...everything a goose hunter could ever hope to need in his pursuit of success afield; everything, that is, except some advice on what to do with all this stuff once it's in the field or on the water. But how to offer up these suggestions *without* the need for a separate and entire book on strategies? As those of you who have made it this far may have already discovered, Canada geese alone could well necessitate a full-length, single species project. Regarding white geese, at least two books are already in existence, and I'm sure as this Spring Conservation Order plods along, additional guides – literary and human both – will come into being. Speckle-bellies? Well, it just hasn't happened yet, but that's not to say that there's not enough material to warrant *Strategies for Specks*, or something like that.

That all said, I come back full circle to the question – How to pass along these goose hunting tactics and techniques without rewriting *War and Peace*? Here's what I came up with. You assemble a squadron of some of the best-known, most efficient goose hunters – that's all-round hunters…not just callers or blind-builders or decoy makers or whatever – roaming the United States today, and you ask them, plain and simple, what it takes to successfully and consistently kill birds under typical as well as atypical field conditions. You want to know how to do it? These guys *know* how to do it.

Canadas by the calendar

Let's start off with Canada geese, a not surprising place to begin seeing as these are the birds that the vast majority of the country is familiar with. Not that snows and blues and white-fronts don't have their following – they do; however, everyone, or at least damn near everyone, wants to know how to kill what's known in the vernacular as *honkers*, undeniably the big game animal of the goose hunter's world.

But it seemed that there was more to hunting Canadas than simply hunting Canadas. And then it hit me. The calendar. Sure, everybody and his brother – All right, almost everybody – can go out on 1 September and shoot into a limit of resident Canada geese, but take this same man using the same early season tactics and fast-forward into the middle of December, and what do you have? A guy who's cold, frustrated, and owns one of the cleanest shotguns east OR west of the Mississippi River. Why clean? Hell, he hasn't shot it since September 10, that's why.

So my point? My point is Canadas by the Calendar. That is, what it takes to change with the seasons and stay as effective a goose hunter throughout December and January as you were during those warm, buggy days in early September. Here's how –

Early geese with Scott Trienen

The Pro – Julie and I met Scott Trienen at the 2003 Avery International goose calling championship in southern Illinois, and quickly determined that you'd be hard-pressed to meet a nicer kid. Twenty-two years old and a resident of Minnesota where he cut his goose hunting eyeteeth on some of the toughest geese in the country, the legendary Rochester area, Trienen has been guiding goose hunters in his home state for the past five years. The young man is also an accomplished competitive caller, with wins that include the 2002 Galyans' Open and the '02 Minnesota State title. In his *spare* time, he's a catcher for the Mahoning Valley Scrappers, a farm team of the Cleveland Indians – GO TRIBE! Here's what this young man has to say about hunting early Canadas, or as they're affectionately known – The Birds of Summer.

The biggest misconception about early Canadas – That they're gonna be real easy, and that the geese are on a schedule. More people are doing this early season. The

Scott Trienen – guide, competitive goose caller, minor league baseball catcher, and nice kid. What Trienen has to say about the early season is interesting.

birds are wising up faster. It only takes a couple days for that old gander to get smart or smarter.

Here's a story. It's opening day early season for the Thompson Family. They have the chopped cornfield. It's a gimme hunt. They get together and clean up all their decoys. They brush up their blind. Start with a combination of full-bodies, shells, silhouettes, whatever. Opening day, it's the opening-day ritual. They have the blinds looking perfect, and 100 or 150 decoys in a junkyard spread. The first flock comes out – 30 birds. Dad picks up his flute call, and the kid tries something on his new short-reed. The geese know nothing, so they come right in and the guys shoot, say, four on the first pass. They're all excited. They make all this noise, and these four young ones come back and they kill them all. There's now birds flying all over the place, and it goes on like this all morning. By the time it's over, they've killed their 25 birds.

I'm telling you this because it's 80 percent of goose hunters on opening morning. These guys are educating a lot of birds. They're educating them for the later part of the season. I'm not saying don't go hunt. I'm trying to explain maybe how to hunt these early season birds in such a way that you're not educating the masses, and you're not making it so hard on yourself for the latter part of the season. What you do in the early season IS going to affect what you do in the latter part of the season. What I want to try to prevent are these early season hunters handing these geese their diplomas on the very first day of the season.

Early season decoy spreads don't need to be big to be effective; in fact, smaller rigs are often more productive, and leave you something for later.

I'm a *h-u-g-e* fan of hiding in the standing corn, especially in the early season. If it's available, use it.

Phil Bourjaily killed this early season Ohio Canada over a small (12) spread and with very little calling, both preferred tactics during this time.

Make those birds work for it.

Scouting the early season – I'm looking at six different things. One, the night roost, which is typically a larger body of water. Two, the field or fields that they're using. Three, what I call their day beds – where they're sitting during the day. This might be a river or a farm pond, but chances are it's going to have pasture or something like it around it so they can graze. Four, the fly routes or flight lines. Where are these birds coming from and going to, and *how* are they flying...low, high, cruising. Five is their behavior on the ground; that is, what they're doing in the fields. Are they lounging in the field? Feeding? Using that field for takeoff and landing practice for the little ones? This will determine whether or not this is a field I want to concentrate on. And six, the weather. Most of all in the early season, the weather is really going to dictate what these birds do, if they do anything.

Decoys, and the early season - I usually start with only six. They can be silhouettes, shells, anything. I'm going to save my most realistic decoys for later. As long as what I'm doing is working, I'm not going to show any more of my hand than I have to. Maybe I'll go to 12. I purposely hunt sloppy. I'll use dirty decoys. It's early in the season, and these birds will decoy to that.

Residents or locals are very family-oriented, and tend to keep to themselves. So I'm using fewer decoys and spread them out more. But understand that you need to read the geese, and change as the birds change. And start

Mid-season can mean tough, frustrating birds, but that doesn't mean that it's time to quit. Rather, it's time to adapt.

small and build in terms of decoys. I hardly ever get above 24 decoys, and I haven't had to use my full-bodies yet. I try to save my most realistic spread for later.

Again, I like the tight knit family groups that are real spread out. Usually a sentry or two in each group with the rest feeding. I try to stay real basic, and don't try to do anything fancy.

Early-season blinds – Is there a tree line I can set up in? A cornfield or a fence line? Standing corn is my favorite. Anything natural that I can set up along on that outer ring of the field I've scouted. I don't immediately run out to the center of the field and set up. These geese are going to be uneducated for a while, and you can get away with some of this stuff. And if you can do this without using a layout blind, then you have that to go with later in the season. You want to save your ground blinds. When these geese figure out that they're constantly getting shot at the edge of the fields and move into the middle, that's when you pull out your ground blinds and move into the middle.

Usually I don't stubble my layout blinds immediately. I just let the camouflage pattern do the job, or I just stubble it a little bit. Then you can camouflage it up a little bit more each time. As the birds get tougher, your camouflage gets a little more intense.

Calling – I like a call that has a lot of volume during the early season because a lot of times I'm not hunting right where the geese want to be. Usually this is a higher-pitched call so it carries and has the volume I need to be

able to reach those geese. I may be close to the flight line but not right underneath. I like to set up on the EDGE of the flight line or fly route, not directly underneath, and call them to me. That's why I like a high volume call. Something where they're going to hear you. On windy days, I call a little more. On rainy days when they're flying low and quiet, I do less calling. The key now is to be real simple with your calling.

I like having two guys call. We'll honk and cluck back and forth. Just real simple. Two birds talking. One guy will be a little deeper, like the old gander, and they other guy will be higher-pitched.

We don't like to use the comeback and pleading calls in the early season, and that goes back to this showing your entire hand theory. If we need to get a bird to turn around, we'll just get real excited. Fast clucks. Fast double-clucks. Everybody's pleading at them, and the longer I can save this type of calling, the better it's going to be on me. Just like decoys and blinds, you don't have to get fancy with your calling until the birds do. Act like the geese do. Geese don't do a lot of pleading and moaning early in the season. They're keeping to themselves and doing their own thing. Be simple with them. Save your best calling stuff for when the birds pull out their best stuff.

Hunting over water – It goes back to the education thing. If you're hunting resident geese and they're using little water holes, it's going to be very effective to hunt

Smaller spreads and watching what your neighbor's doing – and doing something different – are just two of the many mid-season strategies that can spell success.

those holes. I think geese are easier to decoy on water 'cause that's where they want to be. They feel safe there. There's less hunting pressure. But the education level really jumps when you hunt them over water in this early season. And when you do this, these birds are going to move. First, they might move to another body of water. Then you shoot them up there. Then they move into the city limits or into a refuge, like we have here. And these birds then aren't going to fly back out into the country so you can shoot at them. They're going to land on football fields. On soccer fields. On baseball fields. On industrial park fields. And you're left waiting for new geese who don't know the program. When you hunt water in the early season, you're really burning the candle at both ends.

George Lynch on mid-season Canadas

The Pro – I had the pleasure of meeting Mister George Lynch in southern Iowa in the winter of 2003. A quiet man, save for those times he spoke of geese, Lynch talked highly of those he knew and admired in the industry – Grounds, Zink, and the like. At 44, though you'd never guess it, Lynch is the owner of the interestingly named *Lynch Mob Calls*. Motto? "If you want to hang them low, get a Lynch Mob." And by THEM, Lynch means geese. Lots of them. Career-wise, Lynch has recently shifted gears, and has joined forces with Aaron Volkmar and his central

Iowa-based Folded Wings Guide Service, where he'll be working with waterfowl clients in Iowa, Missouri, Minnesota, and Connecticut. Over coffee one morning in December, I talked with Lynch about the strategies used to snooker Canadas in the middle of the season –

The definition of mid-season - I'd define the mid-season as that period when you're still shooting the locals, but you haven't gotten the bulk of the flight birds yet. You're getting a few flight birds every time you have two or three days of north winds. I'll get on the Internet and keep track of the winds with the Weather Channel. I really like to see those north winds, or else you're still hunting those same old birds that have been banged at since September.

Lynch on adaptation – Guys aren't being mobile now. They're not changing. They're not being adaptable. They think 'cause they're seeing the birds, they're going to be shooting the birds. They're underestimating the birds. I'm telling them – 'Guys, these geese have seen the deal. They know what's going on. They're seeing the same thing every day. You got to change up.'

Being adaptable means being aware of what's going on around you. Being able to look at your situation and then changing things up. Having different types of decoys, for one. You're got to get on the ball and scout and hunt different locations. You change the number of decoys you're using. You hunt water instead of the fields. And one of the biggest things is guys not letting fields rest.

Natural movement, says Lynch, is the key to killing mid-season birds. Shells on *wobble stakes* are just one way of imparting that natural movement.

Mid-season decoys – In the early part of the season, you see guys mixing up their decoys. They're putting full-bodies with shells with silhouettes, and they'll have some success. The geese are just seeing goose bodies in the field. They haven't been hammered. When it comes to the mid-season, I NEVER-NEVER-NEVER mix decoys. It's not very realistic. If I'm using silhouettes, I'm using all silhouettes. If I'm using full-bodies, I'm using ALL full-bodies. And the only time I'm using shells is when I'm hunting on snow or on the ice.

If there's one key decoy, and I think that Fred (Zink) will tell you the same thing, it's my sentry decoy. He's the eye-catcher. He's the one I strategically place where I want those geese to land. He's the one adding realism to the spread. It used to be that you used one sentry to every dozen decoys or so. I might have 3 or 4 sentries per dozen. I call them the coyote watchers. These are the ones that when you drive by a field of geese, he's got his head up. He's already seen you. And he's NOT looking at you with eyes in the back of his head. He's turned to face you. You watch geese as they go to land with other geese. Those sentries on the ground will turn to face those incoming birds, and they'll start up an aggressive clucking.

The other guys – It makes a lot of sense to look around and see what the other guys are using. Everybody's using Eliminators and goose chairs and Bigfoot decoys. Use something different. It's a new age of goose hunting, and you can't go out there with the same thing every day and expect to be consistent. You have to be aware of what's going on around you, not only with the geese but what the other guys are doing as well.

The importance of natural movement – I've seen birds get spooky to flagging. I've seen flags flare birds. Just movement alone isn't the key anymore. These birds have seen it, and they've seen it all. It's NATURAL movement. If it looks like your decoy's doing the Moonwalk or some sort of dance, that isn't natural movement. I like windsocks. Guys keep forgetting about the basics, like windsocks. We think that we have to be high-tech. Just because it's moving doesn't mean it's natural movement. Those head-bobbles that you can put on your decoys? I think those are awesome, if it's not too windy. Guys will laugh at me, but I'll take the old windsocks and use white spray paint on the butt of those socks. And I'll over-emphasize that white 'cause that's what those geese are locking in on. Think about looking at geese in a field. What you notice is that white butt waddling back and forth. I'll use 3 or 4 of these windsocks with my sentries, and put them where I want those geese to be.

Over water – There's roosting ponds and there's holding ponds. Roosting ponds are typically your bigger water where the birds stay at night. These geese will fly out in the morning to feed, and then they won't go back to the roost pond, but they'll go to what I call a holding area. A cattle pasture pond, golf courses. Just smaller ponds where the birds are holding up during the day.

Ron Latschaw refers to late-season Canadas as veterans. They've seen it all, so you have to show 'em something different.

Think of a triangle formed by the roost pond, a holding pond, and a fielding feed. If I can find any water inside that triangle, I'll really key on that. Maybe I'll set some full-bodies on the shore and some floaters in the water. Or if I can find 3 or 4 of these holding ponds, and hunt back and forth between them. You don't want to overhunt them.

Ron Latschaw discusses late-season Canadas

The Pro – Before I met Ron Latschaw, I would have said that anyone known as Mister Eliminator had to – HAD TO – be a card-carrying member of the World Wrestling Federation. But that, as they say, was then, and while I still can't imagine Latschaw made up to look like Gene Simmons and stalking the ring in neon-orange stretch shorts, I *can* see the man and the revolution that his company, Final Approach, brought to goose hunting in the form of his *Eliminator* low-profile blind being very synonymous terms. That was in 1993, the year that the southern Oregon resident rocked the goose world, and he's been at it ever since.

Today, Latschaw remains on the cutting edge of innovation in terms of hiding from and successfully hunting Canada geese all across the country, so it made sense to plague him with a series of phone calls and questions regarding something a lot of folks want to know…the *how*

of late season Canadas –

Latschaw defines late season Canadas – I'd say that today, there's even late season geese in Canada. Here, I'm talking resident geese that are born there and don't really leave there unless they're totally pushed out by weather. The Regina area has a hell of a population of resident geese. Those birds can be called late season geese because they're hunted from Day One – September 1 – until the end of the season, and I think that's December 31. Those geese get hard to hunt after three weeks of hunting pressure. Any bird that's been through that gauntlet – come into a decoy spread and seen the guns going off and see birds fall…you know, had the fear of God put in them that way…they start getting smart quick. And they don't have to have it happen 10 or 12 times.

Late season, to me, basically means veterans. Geese that have seen what's going on. They've been through the mill.

Scouting changes – The biggest thing now is that I'm really cautious in the way I approach fields. You know there may be 150 to 200 geese using a field, and you don't know they're there because you can't see them because of how the terrain lays. So I'm real cautious about how I approach this field. I never drive out into the fields – never. I stay completely away, and do all my looking with binoculars, if I can. Those late season birds are spooky. They're in the survival mode. They have their scouts or their sentinels that are real wary. And it only takes one set

These big Ohio Canadas were hitting the fields hard this snowy December morning; however, they weren't doing it until 10 o'clock.

of eyes to see something they don't like. I've had birds lift off a field 500 yards away and fly off…and I know it was me that scared them. When you're scouting, you're hunting. And I can't say this cautious thing enough.

Weather and geese – Weather has a big role to play with these late season geese. If the weather's decent – cold, a little front, a 10 mile-per-hour breeze, but decent – the honkers, the big geese, tend to come out a little later. If you're hunting a field that has both honkers and lessers or smaller geese using it, the lessers will almost be done flying before the honkers start coming out. I mean there may have been an hour and a half flight of lessers into that field before you ever see a big goose. When you get into the serious weather, the snowstorms and stuff, I've had it happen both ways. They'll come out early on ya, and they'll come out late on ya. Hell, sometimes it'll be 1:00 in the afternoon before they fly.

Morning versus evening hunts – I will hunt in the evenings, but I try not to. When those birds get to that point and you do shoot them out in the evening, you don't have anything for the next morning at all. You're scouting is over with, or worse, you're driving around in the dark trying to find a hunt for the next morning.

On being adaptable – You gotta play the game the way the birds want to play the game. You're playing on their terms always, I think. When those resident geese have been beat up so bad you can hardly hunt them, that's when I start getting tactical. Super-small decoy spreads.

Late-season decoys – More than anything else, my spreads are changing by numbers. I put out 8 decoys. That's kind of my magic number. A lot of people think I'm lying when I say it, but I tell you what, I've had some of the best shoots I've ever had over decoys over just 8 decoys. One reason is that when geese commit and come into a spread of 8 decoys, they're right there. I mean everybody's going to have a shot at them. You're not all spread across the decoy spread. You put out 100 decoys, and those birds can land on the left side. They can land on the right side. It's magic when they come into eight decoys. They've had it. There's no getting away from you.

I'll put out Bigfoot decoys, for instance. Three feeders, four sentinels, and maybe one rester. That's it. One rester, three heads down and four heads up. It looks like a small family group, again in that survival mode, that are standing off by themselves. They're not getting into a big group of birds 'cause they're cautious. And it's interesting that the birds that are cautious and are in the bigger groups themselves find these small decoy groups really interesting, and they come right down to them.

A disadvantage? I don't think so 'cause if there were that many flight birds in the area, you wouldn't set up this way anyway. You'd be setting up for the flight birds. That's what your guy – NOTE: See George Lynch above – is talking about when he talks about being adaptable. About rolling with the punches. You have to adapt to each and every situation. The geese over here around Burns,

Hunting on the edge, blending in, changing your blinds – Whatever it takes during the late season. And don't be shy about experimentation.

Latschaw suggests small – 8 decoys!! – but very realistic spreads during the late season in keeping with this Do Something Different theory.

Oregon, are getting pounded from September 1 through January 31, and they're tough. They're tougher than hell. But this is the formula that seems to work for me.

Hunting on the edge – Another thing is getting out into the middle. You know during the late season, we've killed tons of geese hunting on the edge. We'll sit on a fencerow or a hedgerow that's running halfway out into the middle of a field. It looks like a point. And we'll get out there and put our 8 decoys out, say, 25 yards. We're using our blinds 'cause the blinds blend real well with the fence lines. And they're low, too.

We're doing a new video with some guys from Boise that will be out in 2004 that's called *On the Edge*. And it's all hunting from the edge of the fields. It's an instructional deal that talks about things like wind direction because wind direction is critical. It really is when you're hunting these edges. Using the blinds 'cause they keep you low and they blend so well. We hunted seven days for this video, and in those seven days we killed 287 geese hunting on the edge.

There's a science to it, though, and it's not just a gimme. You gotta know which direction the flights are coming from. That's important. The wind is WAY important so you know which side of the field to set up in. These guys started doing this when they were hunting turf farms. Hell, there's no way you're going to set up in the middle of a turf farm. That grass is an inch tall, and those late season birds will pick those out like crazy. So they

Contest routines sound great on the stage, but for the most part, they're out of place in the field...especially during the *Low Call or No Call* late season.

went to the edges where the irrigation ditches were and there was a little taller grass, and just killing them. They'd put 11 or 12 blinds out.

Late-season blinds – When you're hunting on these edges, you're covering the blinds up. I mean really covering them up. You're using tumbleweeds or whatever, but you're basically covering the whole blind up. I'm using this *Whoop Grass* (Kolpin Outdoors) around the head holes of the blinds. It covers up my face, but I can still see through it. And nothing's poking me in the eyes. But anyway, you're covering up on the edges. You're not trying to blend in like you would in an open-field type of situation. Myself, I put maybe half the cover on the blinds that most people do when I'm out in the middle. I'm just trying to break the blind up and make it look three-dimensional. Most guys cover it up and try to make it look like a pile of hay, and that's the first thing a bird sees. The blinds are supposed to hide the hunter. You're not supposed to hide the blind.

Ron on calling – I back way off on everything, and get real subtle. I don't do the long honks for the distance, but if I know the birds are coming to the field, I'll just honk and cluck. Real quiet and real subtle. Not repetitious at all, and I leave a lot of space between notes. If they're coming, I let them come. Maybe a confidence double cluck, or something like that. Or a moan just to keep them coming. But I never-never try to overdo it 'cause you'll blow them out. The biggest reason is, and I gotta say this

'cause it's important, is that 8 geese on the ground – NOTE: Remember Ron's 8-goose decoy spread? – don't make much noise. There's no flock talk going on. And you gotta remember that. And the other thing you gotta remember is not to call when those birds are straight up over you. It's not going to sound right with that sound coming from the blind and your decoys 25 yards downwind. Those birds are gonna locate you because the sound's coming from you and not the decoys.

So that takes us through the calendar from Opening Day in September to the end of the season, whether that be late November or early December as is the case in the Upper Midwest or the 1 February closure enjoyed by the folks in the west Central and Pacific flyways....lucky bastards.

But wait. There's still more Canadas to come.

The little ones, with Bill Saunders

The Pro – To live and hunt geese in Washington and *not* know of Bill Saunders ranks right up there with living west of the Cascades and not owning a raincoat. It just ain't done, at least not by smart folk. A full-time waterfowl guide, Saunders, 30, is perhaps best known as a maker of custom goose calls, including such notables as his *Traffic, I-5 KLR, Reload*, and the *G.P.*, which by the way, stands for Goose Pimp...but I'll let you ask Bill about that one. To date and by his count, Saunders has entered 14

Good friend, Roger Sparks, sets a small combination water-sandbar island spread in the middle of Colorado's South Platte River, a hotspot for late-season Canadas.

Bill Saunders working his magic on a flight of what a lot of folks refer to as *little geese*. Just 'cause they're little doesn't mean they're easy...eh, Bill?

individual calling contests, and emerged top 'o the heap in an amazing 10 of those, among them the 2003 Idaho Open, 2002 Final Approach Open, 2002 Washington State title, and the 2002 Idaho State Team, which he won with partner, Travis Reeser, and proved that he indeed plays well with others. Saunders currently lives in Kennewick, Washington, with his wife, Lorri, and daughters, Kelsie, 7, and Amanda, 4. He also guides full-time for Mike Franklin's *Pacific Wings Waterfowl Service*, a role he's maintained for the past six seasons. Here's Bill to talk about hunting little Canadas –

NOTE: While, here, Saunders is speaking primarily of his hunting in the West and Pacific Northwest, that's not to say that these techniques can't be used successfully on the smaller subspecies in the Central and Mississippi flyways. Just keep that in mind.

The differences – True lessers, occasional cacklers and westerns – those are the primary ones we have out here. The major difference is in their voices, from the highest-pitched goose to a middle-of-the-road goose in the lesser. Westerns are the largest geese we hunt in the Basin.

It seems like the smaller birds, they stick to larger flocks. The honkers stick to their own kind, and usually to smaller bunches. The lessers stick to bigger bunches. Lessers usually like to have something that's a little more open, a little bigger. And this is the thing about spending as much time in the field as I have. While these birds do have their individual tendencies, I can think back on a

Snow goose spreads are no longer just about quantity, says Toye. You gotta have quantity AND quality today to fool these sharp birds.

hunt for lessers that were in a little boxed canyon. There were so many trees around it, you'd never thought a bird could work its way in there. More often than not, lessers will get themselves in an open area. They'll spend more time on rises. Honkers? Sometimes you'll find them in places you'll never think of finding a goose. It's hard for me to say because I've seen so many different situations.

Saunders on calling – On lessers, I usually spend more time on the high side. Your call is going to be higher-pitched. More often than not, you're going to be calling more aggressively. Definitely faster. Clucking and high-pitched honking, with high-pitched cries. With honkers, a lot more on the low side – clucking, moaning, and lots of growls.

Cries, and more calling – Cries are a moan that I call a cry. When you hear lessers, it's a higher-pitched moan. You can call it a yelp. When I think of a yelp, I think of something that has a definite ending. A cry is more...it just fades out. It might be one of my own terms, but a cry is what I'm saying a lesser does instead of moaning. Like turkey hunting or anything, some days different is going to work. A different sound may be the key to getting the bird. There's days when I'll use these cries with a couple clucks thrown in, and they'll just bomb in. And I said that you want to call hard and fast for lessers – and volume, too – but there's days when no calling or just high-pitched clucks work real well. You can kinda generalize what these birds do, but if you ask the guys who've been out there,

Water hunting Canadas IS a lot of work; however, the pay-offs can be as big as the hunting is hard.

Julie gunning snows near Russell, Manitoba, Canada. Believe me, the birds up there are no less wary than they are once they arrive in The States.

It doesn't matter – Spring or Fall – killing adult white geese in this day and age is an achievement worthy of merit. Just ask the guy who hunts 'em!

there's nothing set in stone. And that's why I can do it every day because it's different every day.

A word on pitch – I do think a high-pitched call makes a difference when calling to the smaller geese. They want to hear what they're used to. They want to hear Mama. But I use a high-pitched call on honkers, too. Until I started making calls, I lived and died by Tim Grounds' Half Breed. I thought it was the best call out there, and it probably still is one of the best field calls. It was effective on the biggest honkers you could find, and it's a high-pitched call. Birds – turkeys, ducks, geese, whatever – they seem to respond well to that high-pitched sound.

Decoys, and the little ones – If I'm out there and I know specifically that I'm going to be dealing with lessers, I usually pull my spread in a little bit tighter than I would with honkers. I mean tighter to one another. They usually are a little bit closer to each other. They usually set more in a ball. Honkers, as they feed, will stretch out a bit. In the morning, when lessers hit a field, they'll usually ball up pretty good. But with honkers in the morning, when they first hit a field, some will hit here and there. There'll be some space between them. My spread for lessers – some guys call it the Dunkin Donut – is just a ball of decoys with a hole in the middle. And those lessers will try to pile right into that hole. And it's deadly. Big flocks or small flocks, it works on both.

The last five years, I've used exclusively honker stuffers. But this year, I'm switching to a spread of lesser

Basic whites – jackets, pants, plus a little camouflage to blend in – are still the mainstay of many a spring snow goose hunter.

decoys. They're carved after lessers. They're the Hardcore decoys. I've ordered 120 lessers and 30 honkers, and that's what I'm going to be using this year. I doubt if I set them all every time. When I hunt over stuffers, I hunt over 50 to 75 taxidermy birds. It's relying on a small spread of realistic decoys as opposed to a great big black spot – you know, all the shells and silhouettes and Bigfoots, and you wail on the calls and try to muscle them in. I guess you could say that my style of hunting leans more to the realistic side of things.

A final note – I call hard and aggressive, but that's kind of my ace in the hole. I try to get it done with as little calling and as small a rig as possible. As the season wears on and the birds get tougher, I can pull out more decoys or start calling a little harder. Most guys show them all their cards right from the beginning of the season and try to get it done doing that right 'til the end. And that doesn't work. I tried it when I was younger. I would set everything I had and I would call like a madman at every flock, and toward the end of the season, you don't have anything to throw at them.

Tommy Stutzman on Canadas over water

The Pro – You know, I can't even recall where nor when I met Tommy Stutzman. But I will say that without question, he's one of the most enthusiastic – and most realistic – goose hunters I've ever had the pleasure of crossing paths with. Now 36, though he'll say and perhaps wish 23, Stutzman is the owner of Central Flyway Game Calls located – Ready for this? – in Beaver Crossing, Nebraska. By his own admission, Tommy "loves Canadas," but that's not to say you won't find him sitting along his beloved Platte River behind a mallard spread…though I'm sure there'll be a plastic Canada in the woodpile somewhere. Less than a year after picking up his first goose call in September of 1993, Stutzman amazed listeners, and himself, by winning the Missouri State goose calling championship. In 1998, he'd walk away with the World Snow Goose calling title, and it's been a wild, nonstop ride ever since.

Here, Tommy talks about one of his favorites – hunting big Canadas over water.

Stutzman on scouting – I don't have access to 32 miles of river, but what I'm looking for in these types of rivers like the Platte is shallow water. Something where I can see the bottom, and walk in hip boots or less. And open. I'm not afraid to hunt around trees, but a goose prefers to be where they can see. Some place that won't or can't hide predators. And islands, so you can load those sandbar islands up with full-bodied decoys and load the water up with floaters.

The biggest mistake – The biggest mistake I see guys constantly making has to do with impatience. Blow three notes on your call and the goose makes two passes, not

Says Toye, electronic callers – E-callers – aren't a magic bullet, but can be a valuable tool in the snow hunter's arsenal.

getting closer with either one, so you whack at 'im. And do nothing more than educate him. Today's hunting, I think, takes a lot more self-discipline. Be more concerned about doing it right.

A day on the water – A typical day on the Platte River is shoot a few ducks in the morning. And by in the morning, I'm talking about right at shooting light. Maybe you'll have an hour of that, and then it's going to slow down. An hour later, and your ducks are going to be coming back from the fields. About the time the ducks are coming back, the geese are waking up and getting ready to head out. Hopefully they're going to be in small groups. But the geese will go out to feed, and then – at least on the Platte – it's going to be 10:30 to 11:30, and those birds are going to come back to water. Anybody who would leave the river before noon is nuts.

Stutzman discusses decoys – I run both full-bodies and floaters. The Platte may only be ankle deep, but there's some current running through there. How are you going to anchor floaters? Sometimes we put stakes on the feet of our full-bodies and stake those in the shallows. I do pay attention to my anchor lines and anchors. It's pretty cut and dried. If my spread looks stupid to me…if it doesn't look right, why should it look any better to a goose? Use brown cord and step on your weights to bury them in the sand. And if I don't like the way it looks, I'll retie the entire rig.

In an island situation, I'll use resting decoys. But it depends on what you're doing. A goose that's coming back

to the river after feeding in the morning isn't going to immediately hit the water and take a nap. So my decoys are 'awake,' but relaxed. On an afternoon shoot, I'll probably go with some resters. Heads tucked back. Take the feet off your full-bodies and put them right on the sand. Simple things like that.

Where I am, the more floaters the better. Why? Because nobody does it. They'll load the bank up and load the little island up, and that's about it. Me, I'd just as soon give the birds a totally different look than what everyone else is doing. With floaters, you get that natural movement. They're moving instead of just sitting there.

Calls on the water – I think geese over water, birds that are coming back from feeding anyways, do a lot more moaning. In a field situation, geese seem to do more excited clucks and honks, but over water, it's more relaxed or mellow. More moans and deeper honks. Regardless of whether it's fields or water, every day I'm trying to figure out what the geese want to hear. And you don't know what that is, but you try to figure that out. And you just know. When you hit that note and you're watching the birds' body language and they tell you that you have what they want to hear. Maybe it's just one or two or three birds, but you don't need them all.

Over the water on those calm, blue days? I'm not afraid to hunt those days, but your calls can be overbearingly loud. Have you ever heard a goose echo? I haven't, and on these types of days, you can hear yourself call six

White-fronts, aka specks, are wonderful birds; unfortunately, folks just don't have access to these amazing and very unique geese.

miles downstream. Is there anything you can do? Not really, though one thing I do is never go to the field with only one call. I don't limit myself that way. In those situations, I'll have a call that for me is tuned deeper and I won't blow it as loud. I won't call as often

Canadas over water, with Barnie Calef

The Pro – Barnie Calef is the kind of guy you don't mind sharing a blind with. He's pretty handy with a shotgun, knows his way around a boat blind, and enjoys drinking a beer – or several – when the ducks are dressed and the guns are put away for the evening. The fact that he's the – THE – three-time world duck calling champion doesn't hurt none neither. Knowing that one of Calef's favorite places in the world is that flat expanse of cattail-studded Missouri River near Yankton, South Dakota, a place known for both hoards of red-legged mallards and heavyweight Canadas, I asked him, a fellow Iowan, to the house one evening to get his thoughts on the subject of hunting big geese over water – a sort of icing to Stutzman's cake. In between sips on a cold Budweiser and complaints that I was contributing to the downfall of his diet, the three-time champ, who's not too shabby on a short reed himself, had this to say –

Why not water – Labor-intensive is one reason more people don't hunt geese over water. Water spreads for

geese are a lot of work. We'll put out maybe 30 or 40 Bigfoot floaters, and to carry those along with all the duck decoys we need is just cramming those boats full of decoys. Also, guys have always hunted the fields and let the geese have the water to rest and roost. Another reason would be that so many of our refuges include that water. There again, the thinking being to let those geese have the water and then hunt them in the fields. And then I guess that the fourth thing would be opportunity. Up there on the Missouri where we hunt, it's classic mallard and honker water. It's vast and open. Now go somewhere else, and those guys aren't going to have water opportunities like those.

Decoys and placement – We use Bigfoot floaters. Why? Realism. Simple as that. They're just unbelievable. As for head positions and such — if someone asked me to design a goose floater, I'd put together something that was….well, we call them short-neckers. It's just a goose sitting there on the water. I understand the different head positions required in the field because of wanting to create the illusion of motion, but on the water, you're left with the swing of the decoys for your motion – so to me, the head positions don't matter.

To me, decoy placement is critical. And maybe it's just me. Most of my hunting consists of mallards and honkers over water at the same time. What I've realized is to forget the Type A Realistic spread because what you're trying to do is position birds for a shot more than make your spread look like real birds. What I'll do is put out an L – the diagonal over either shoulder, with the honkers on the upwind end out about 40 yards and the ducks trailing on the long arm. That's probably as unrealistic looking as you can be.

Ducks and geese together – There are no steadfast rules when it comes to ducks and geese. About the time you got them figured out, they stump you. The first thing I did was listen to the rule-makers who said to separate your mallards from your honkers. So we'd put our duck decoys, and then put our goose decoys somewhere else. What we noticed immediately was that the mallards were decoying to our honker decoys. It didn't matter where they were. The ducks would go overtop the mallard decoys to land behind the goose decoys. After a couple seasons of beating our heads against the wall, we decided to use this to our advantage. What we did then was to set up the 'L' I mentioned earlier, and the mallards would pitch into the spot where the duck decoys and the goose decoys meet. Without fail.

Calef on calling…geese – Over a water set, I typically stick with honks, clucks, and moans. I don't do much double-clucking. Over a field, those geese are excited. They're pumped 'cause they're coming in to feed, and it seems like they're highly vocal. There, I'll do more excited, fast calling. More of that. The best way I've found and I tell guys to call geese on the water is to honk, and then listen. Cluck, and then listen. If they're answering back, you're doing the right thing. It's pretty simple, really.

Tony Toye, and his blizzard of white

The Pro – During the Fall of 2000 while Julie and I were working on our first in this series, *Successful Duck Hunting*, it was suggested by co-conspirator and fellow Iowan, Phil Bourjaily, that I call Tony Toye and interview him on the subject of hunting divers. Seems Toye, as I was told, specifically targeted canvasbacks on the Mississippi River, and did quite well for himself and the full boat of clients he guided each season as part of his Big River Guide Service. Not only did I call Toye, but my wife and I spent the day with him on the Mississippi – a day at the close of which I walked away not only with my first drake canvasback, but the very valid impression that here was a guy knowledgeable far beyond his then 32 years. Today, now 36, Toye still targets cans on the Mississippi when the USFWS allows; however, the months of February and March will find the Boscobel, Wisconsin resident in the northwest corner of Missouri, dressed in whites and hiding 'neath an oversized white goose decoy while the barking of electronic snows echoes from 8-ohm speakers 'round his position. And the man does it right. In 1997, the first year he hunted what has become known as the

Spring Conservation Season, Toye and his clients recorded 141 white geese. Five years later in 2002, he and his people were responsible for the demise of 3,370 snows, blues, and Ross' geese. That's a lot of tundra being saved!

That said, I'd like to introduce Tony Toye, and his take on success in the spring –

Fall versus spring – For fall snows, you have to be in the field they were in the night before. Scouting is absolutely critical. Setting up in the same field two mornings in a row is suicide. Spring hunting, you find a good spot in the migration path and you can hunt that – and we've done it – 30 days straight. You can have your best days toward the end of the season. It's just totally different, and I think it's a lot easier. In the fall, it seems like it's an all-or-nothing thing. And in the spring, it's a trickle effect. Night and day difference in the migration.

Scouting, and the wind – In the spring, we're looking for a field that offers wide open spaces. Protection for the birds. We know where the flight paths are, and we just try to get underneath them. There are times when the birds are hitting a certain field, and we'll set up that night and have a tremendous hunt the next morning. The same techniques that work in the fall will work in the spring, but we're tending to use a lot bigger decoy spreads in the spring. This allows us to stay in the same fields day after day.

I know guys who move every single day, and we just seem to do better than they do. Some of it, I'm sure, has to do with the fact that we try to hunt water. At least half of our spreads are water, and those can be really hot. You cannot go wrong setting up in a field that the geese used the day before. If it doesn't work, it wasn't because you were in the wrong spot. But it might be a one-shot deal.

Our best days occur on sunny days with a south wind. You can't get any better than that. Fifty to 60 degrees, and good weather to the south of us. We've had days when we've had that good weather but there's been thunderstorms to the south of us, and it hasn't been that good. But if the jetstream is coming from way down south and the weather down south of us is good, it triggers the migration.

Snow decoys in general – In my opinion, more is better. The snows haven't changed in any way, and they're still flying in huge numbers. Until they start breaking up into small family groups like Canadas – laughs – then I'll go to smaller spreads. Our spreads are not only getting bigger, but they're getting better. Guys are going to better decoys, and some are trying the smaller spreads. But I still think that the bigger and better decoys and decoy spreads…it's the only way to go. We're not using rags anymore. We're using Northwinds, floaters, and full-bodies.

We're using 1,500 to 2,000 decoys. Of that, about 90 percent are Northwinds. Of those, about 20 percent are headed Northwinds. Approximately 40 percent of the

Northwinds are juveniles or blues. Does that make a difference? The grey geese? I don't know, but definitely the blue geese. For one, you get away from the spread, and the grey geese just look white. But the blues – one, it snows a lot, and when it snows, they're the only ones that really stick out. When we use full-bodies, we have a little bit of everything – Flatlands, Carrylites, Higdons, Bigfoots.

With a spread that size, we set the blinds last. If we're hunting these fields more than one day, we'll set up for all the wind directions. That is, just a big mass of decoys. And then each day with the wind changes, we'll do a little different configuration. Some little blobs or feeding groups downwind…just something different each day. Our blinds we'll set up last. The blinds are always getting moved.

Toye on decoy placement – It may seem haphazard. Getting out 1,500 decoys is the main chore. Once you've gotten those out, then you can go through them and do your picking up here and there. Making little holes here and there. That's how those geese look and feed. If there's no feed in a 20 by 20 section, there's ain't gonna be a goose in it. So we'll leave openings like that in the spread. Just what we see the real geese doing. I don't necessarily leave an opening though for the birds to land. If those geese are going to land, they're going to land right in the middle of everybody. I think that's kind of over-rated, that leaving an opening. Where they think the food is, that's where they're going to land.

Downwinding yourself – We used to, but anymore we don't. Once in a while, we'll get right on the edge of the spread, but not radically downwind. I think the geese are seeing the hunters. It's not the spread that's spooking them, it's the hunters. So if you bury in good enough, those birds are gonna get into range. We've done it where we've sat 100 yards downwind of the spread, and the birds still did it to us. So I think they're picking us out.

Whites on the water – If the birds have to decoy across the water – if the wind's right – it seems like the birds are so much more relaxed. Whether it's because the birds are keying in on the floaters and they – the decoys – look that much more realistic when the wind's blowing, or the fact that they just don't see the water spreads that often. Or, if they're migrating birds, they want water first, and then feed second.

When I set snow floaters, I pack them in tight. I put them on short lines so they don't bump, and I pack them in tight. I try to use between 100 and 200 floaters, and most of them are Model 96 Herter's. We'll then custom paint the blues and the juveniles. We'll put full-bodies right there in the shallows and along the edges of the water. And then the main part of the spread will be the Northwinds in the middle, and then at the other end, I may put some more full-bodies. As for blind placement, it's best if the wind is at your back going across the water.

Snows and blinds – I still think that one of the best

Many Spring snow goose hunters, Toye included, are combining mouth calling with electronics in hopes of hitting all of the bases. Sometimes it works; sometimes it doesn't.

ways of hiding in a snow spread is wearing a white jacket. You step away from the spread, and those guys just disappear. We mainly, though, use goose chairs and Eliminator style blinds. I don't think the low-profile blinds are a must-have for today's spring snow hunter. If you're hunting a disked field, I think they stick out too much when compared to a goose chair. In those situations and on a sunny morning, those layout blinds, especially if you're hunting seven or eight guys, are giving off some major square shadows. If you're only hunting one or two guys – yeah, then I think you can get away with those shadows. With goose chairs, they're giving off goose-shaped shadows which blend in a lot better than the Eliminator type blinds and their shadows do. And they're BIG shadows, and I think that's their downfall in areas where you can't completely hide them.

Toye talks electronics – Electronic callers have made it easier, but I think there's too many guys out there that rely on it too much. They skimp on other stuff like the number or quality of decoys. They're putting all their eggs in one basket with the E-call, and I think that's a huge mistake. The E-call is an excellent tool, and if used correctly, it can provide you with a lot of shooting.

There are certain tapes. For instance, I'm not big on the Johnny Stewart tape because it's so rhythmic. As soon as I hear it, I can tell you that that's a Johnny Stewart tape. And I think if the geese get burned over that tape time and time again, they can get wise to that. I've made my own

The two-note call or yodel of the specklebelly is, to me, relatively easy to mimic; however, says Haydel, it's all in the timing at which you present your notes.

Photo courtesy of Phil Bourjaily

tape, and we don't let it out to anybody. I'm using 15 to 20 seconds of feeding snows. It is repetition, but it's not that single bird calling over and over and over again. It's a bunch of birds. If you listen to it long enough, you can hear it changing over, but the birds can't pick it up.

We still just use a plain cassette tape due to its durability. We've experimented with the CD callers, and at least the equipment that we had couldn't take the abuse that we gave it. And we've had tremendous luck with the cassette. Right now we're using a Gander Getter with four speakers.

Volume and speakers – You can have the volume on too loud. You can forget to flip the tape and the tape ends when the birds are close. Too loud? With the speakers today, I think you can have it too loud. We use one caller and four speakers, and with that, you can have all the sound coming out of four little spots on the ground. We tend to turn the volume down as the birds get closer; however, it all depends on what the birds are reacting to. If they're vocal, we'll toy with it. If they're not, then we starting experimenting. Some days you have to have it really low, and others, you have to turn it up as loud as it can go.

We'll have one speaker 50 to 75 feet behind us. We have one on either side and slightly behind us, with all three facing up and downwind. And then I have one handheld. When the birds are circling, I try to keep the handheld facing the closest birds possible 'cause those are the birds that you gotta have decoy. As they circle, you have to

follow them with the handheld 'cause the other speakers aren't following them. I mean, if they get behind you and your spread, it becomes almost silent. You have to have SOME sound pointed behind you, or they'll bug out.

Toye and mouth calling – We're mouth calling somewhat, but with as loud as it is, I don't think they can hear me. But let's say the tape runs out, or with some tapes you do have quiet spots, that's when mouth calling is critical.

The line of thinking where everybody gets on a call and makes as much noise as possible is still out there. And that's what it sounds like – noise. Today in the spring, if we get caught off guard with the electronic call, I'll voice call. And when I get a bird answering me, I'll answer them right back. And it's generally one bird that you're calling to.

Rod Haydel on speckle-bellies

The Pro – I caught up with Rod Haydel one morning in December during the heart of south Louisiana's duck season. "Funny you called yesterday," Haydel said. "I was on the road coming back from our marsh in Lake Charles. Had my son with me, and we killed three specks over our duck spread. Should have had our limit – that's six birds – but you know how that goes." Yes, Rod, I do know…all too well.

A young man at 40, Haydel currently sits as president of the family's call company, as well as handles the advertising and public relations aspect for the 1981-vintage firm. Married to his high school sweetheart, he has a duck-hunting son, 18, and a 15-year-old daughter, all of whose prospective suitors know that her Daddy spends much of the year with a shotgun in his hand.

It was in the early 1980s when Haydel fell in love not only with his wife-to-be, but with that wonderful bird called the white-fronted goose. Since that time, Haydel's admiration for the specklebelly has grown to where today, and while he can still be found in fields from Canada to east Texas hunting white geese and honkers, he'll be the first to tell you that he'd just as soon have specks. And with that, Rod Haydel on hunting specklebellies –

Haydel on why more folks don't hunt specks – There's not a whole lot of specks when you compare them to the numbers of Canadas and snows. And two, they're in limited areas. Their coverage or range isn't as great as snows and Canadas. Down in south Louisiana, a specklebelly goose is considered a prized trophy bird. But when you slip across the Texas line, their limits are only one instead of two like it is here, and they're considered just another goose or a bonus goose.

Down here when a guy's going to go out specifically for specklebellies, once they get their limit or feel the hunt is over, then they pack up and go home. They don't wait around to see if any snows will come in. And you may have millions of snows down there at the time. I guess you could say that specklebellies are a way of life to the folks down in south Louisiana.

On the gullible goose – They can be, and then they can be extremely hard to call in. If you catch the right bird that's flying low, those you can usually call in pretty dog-gone easy. With the amount of hunting pressure that we have down in south Louisiana, those specks can be pretty dog-gone spooky. And I guess that's part of the reason why they're given trophy status down there.

Calling and timing – When you have a specklebelly communicating with another speck, either with birds greeting one another on the ground or actually calling to birds in the air to come join the flock, they're going to do a two-note yodel. Basically what you want to do is imitate that two-note yodel, and go back and forth with one goose. It's hard to explain the timing element that's so very important in developing that calling relationship. If you wait too long after the goose calls and then YOU call, the timing isn't right and they'll keep on passing you by. Basically, you want that goose to call, and within one to one-and-a-half seconds, you want to call. Then go back and forth, back and forth.

If that goose is on a direct line to me, this two-note yodeling back and forth is all I'll do…as long as he's continuing to drop in altitude. I'm okay with that. If he maintains a certain level in his altitude and isn't dropping down, then I'll go to some rapid clucking. Usually he'll drop in altitude, and once he levels off, I'll go back to my two-note yodel for a little bit. Then to rapid clucking again. But again, if that goose maintains a certain level – that is, he's not dropping altitude – on his first approach, or if he circles and maintains that same altitude…well, if he's borderline and you feel you can pull the shot off, it's time to shoot 'cause usually all they'll do from that point on is gain in altitude. They may circle one more time, but then they're out of there. Sometimes, though, when you do that rapid clucking I was talking about earlier, you can get those birds excited again and you can actually see the attitude of that bird change a bit. And sometimes he'll get excited and drop in altitude and come on down.

I love it when you go up to Canada and the locals say that you can't call specklebellies. Well, you put this coon ass in a field where there's specklebellies, and I'll show you somethin'.

NOTE – Years ago, I heard Rod's father, Eli, talk of specklebellies making a three-note call as opposed to their typical two-note yodel. According to Eli, this three-note call wasn't a good thing to hear as it generally meant a goose that wasn't going to come close enough to get himself killed. Or it meant a speck that had seen something wrong. Thinking of this, I asked Rod about what his father had said.

The three-note call – That three-note call is just

Many specks are taken on the pass; that is, coming to the call and spread, but not actually finishing. That's not to say they won't, however.

something they'll do. It's a three-tiered sound, and they'll hold that last note just a little bit longer than the rest of them. Just hang on to that last note a little bit longer.

Most of the times that I've heard birds using a three-note sound and you're blowing a two-note yodel behind it, there has not been any occasion that I can remember where I've called that goose in. We get to experimenting from time to time, and the only thing that I have found that will work, and that probably less than 50 percent of the time, on a three-note goose is for YOU to call the three notes. At some point in his approach, he may switch over to a two-note call. When he does that, you need to switch over to the two-note call. Sometime you'll get that goose in, but if they never switch over to a two-note call, you're probably not going to call that goose in.

Rod on calling wrong – I don't think a guy can do things wrong to the point that it's gonna hurt him. I think if a guy learns those two notes on a specklebelly call, he can go out and probably be very effective. There are certain little subtle sounds you can make, especially when you get into your softer clucking, that I feel sounds more realistic and where you might have an edge over someone else. But your basic two-note yodel…if you keep that timing up, that's going to kill 90 percent of your birds.

On the pass – We're taking a lot of our birds on the pass. I will say that I've called plenty of specks to the ground just doing the two notes. That's how I learned by just using those two notes, and it's worked thousands of

Photo courtesy of Phil Bourjaily

If you're going to hunt specks specifically, says Haydel, get yourself some speck decoys. You don't need many, but white-fronts do like white-fronts.

times for me. Over the years we've tried to experiment with different things, and just see how the geese reacted to it. Not doing anything wild, if you know what I mean, but just experimenting with other natural sounds that those birds make to see what effect it has on them. It used to be where all we'd do is the two-note yodel, but we have found that doing some of those rapid clucks have really helped us have an edge in certain situations.

Haydel talks calls – A speck call is a really, really personal type of call. Much more so than a mallard call. Some guys cannot blow as hard to make the call break. Other guys blow extremely hard. Other calls just fit a particular person better. Some of the calls are a little higher-pitched, and some have a little more rasp to them. One of me and my Dad's mentors, who's passed away now, lived down in south Louisiana, and liked his speck calls extremely low-pitched and very raspy. We'd have to tune his calls to the point where we'd split the reed in order to get it that raspy.

Speck decoys – If you're hunting specklebellies, use specklebelly decoys. If I'm hunting Canadas or snows, I always set my specklebelly decoys off to the side in a little family group. Put them off by themselves. And it doesn't take a whole lot of decoys to be effective with specklebellies. It's like I said. We're constantly experimenting with different sounds and different set-ups. And I think that's the key to hunting these birds, and that's to have a different look than the other guys are using. But if you're going out specifically for specks in a rice field or a bean field, I've hunted with no decoys and had good success. I've hunted with one, two, three, but most of the time, it's a half dozen or under.

10
From field to feast

Young Canadas can be excellent on the table; however, young or old, it's all in how they're handled once they hit the ground.

I have a friend. I won't mention his name, but Friend XX hates, absolutely hates, catfish. Yes, he's leery of the spines. Or the stingers, as he calls them. And he's not really fond of the way cats feel, all slippery and slimy. "Kind of like a booger," he'll say…and then gets real quiet when you ask him just exactly how he came to that particular conclusion.

Most of all, though, Friend XX will tell you that catfish are damn near impossible to clean. Between the slime and the stingers and the bones and their weird body structure, catfish, as least according to Friend XX, give you no place to start and no place to finish. "I don't know where to start," he says in a semi-whine. "And mine always look like they've been run through a Cuisinart. Plus," he continues, "I'm sure as hell not going to eat something that looks like that."

So, on those oh-so-traumatic occasions when Friend XX does indeed hook up with a nice bullhead, channel cat, or flathead, the Gerber Multi-Pliers get quick-drawn and the fish, without so much as a fingertip being laid upon his slick sides, gets turned loose. Friend XX, the unfortunate man, has no idea just how good a fresh-from-the-water channel catfish can be when it's released into a cast-iron skillet filled with 350-degree cooking oil. Poor guy.

What's my point here? My point is this – There are a lot of folks out there who feel about geese as Friend XX does about the fine-eating whiskered things swimming about our nation's rivers. Not that a Canada, speck, or snow's going to sting them or slime them. No, what I'm talking about is the cleaning process, which should then be followed immediately by the eating process. "Geese are big," they'll tell you. "Where do you start?" Or – "Well,

My way of thinking, geese are a hell of a lot easier to clean than catfish. Especially 'cats like this 48-pound Iowa flathead. That's a lot of catfish!

I've had geese a time or two, and I just don't like it. Tasted like rancid liver. Rubber rancid liver."

Now I'm not going to say that every goose I've eaten since my first one in 1979 left me drooling like one of Pavlov's dogs. They haven't. I've had my share of bad culinary experiences. Barbequed goose legs and thighs were a error of judgment on my part. Mature snow goose breasts on the grill? Another experiment that should never have left my brain. Nor gotten there in the first place. Still, I've had countless incredible dining experiences where goose flesh was the guest of honor. In fact, I'll take every honker, white front, or blue that I can get my grubby little paws on. And as for those poor tasters? Well, maybe I just didn't, as Duck Commander Phil Robertson preaches, use enough garlic.

And what about this cleaning thing? Any truth to the fact that preparing that big Canada for the table is nothing short of a Herculean task? I don't think so. Certainly, geese – even the smaller species like Cacklers and Ross' – are some of the largest fowl that a wingshooter will ever encounter on the cutting board; however, here at least, size really doesn't matter at all. The trick, at least in my book, is to find a cleaning method that works for you. Something that you're comfortable with. Maybe you'll find that any one of several different methods can get the job done, and done well. Then it's just a matter of deciding (a) how much time you have for the cleaning process, and (b) what you plan to do with the finished product, as each of

these variables can make a difference in the way the birds are prepared for the table.

But, before we get into all that, I'd like to take a look at the different species of geese available to the North American waterfowler, and how certain folks rate those birds on the table. The results, as you'll see, are rather interesting.

The species on the table

Ask a duck hunter which one he'd rather eat – a widgeon, or a merganser – and chances are, unless he's demented or a HUGE fan of sardine-stuffed grackle, he'll take the baldpate every time. For any number of reasons, diet being without question first and foremost, some ducks just taste better than others. Sure, there are guys out there who'll tell you that coots or shovelers or the aforementioned fish-duck are some of the finest-eating birds available. And that may be true, but if you check, these, too, are the men with cupboards filled with spices – garlic! – marinades, and other…well, I'll just call them masking agents.

It's the same with geese. Some birds, and specklebellies come immediately to mind, are just simply fantastic on the table. Specks, I do believe, could be dragged behind a honey wagon in south Louisiana for eight days during August, thrown on the grill, and still have you coming back asking for seconds and thirds. They're just that way. On the other hand, my experiences with white geese have been rather lackluster; other folks, though, have recipes for snows and blues that will get your mouth watering from a distance of 200 yards. Canadas? I've had Canadas to die for, and some that I just think flat died.

Curious about what other folks thought, I decided to ask around and get the straight skinny on what I'll call the Tale of the Tastebud Tape.

Canadas – I like Canadas. Not the big honking – translation: big and old – birds that have seen both ends of the flyway eight to 12 times, but the younger birds. The ones just a couple years old. And especially those that I'll call the grey geese, the birds hatched in late April or May that decoy so well during many states' early-September dark-goose season. *Those*, now, I like real well.

"I like Canadas. Sure, it depends on where they're roosting and what they're eating, but I like 'em," says Tommy Stutzman, former world champion snow goose caller and owner of Central Flyway Game Calls in Beaver Crossing, Nebraska. "One thing with geese, actually all game but most importantly geese, is that you just don't butterfly it, wrap it around an onion with bacon, and throw it on the grill with some sauce expecting it to taste just like the last Porterhouse steak you had. There needs to be some preparation involved," he continued. "Add some seasoning. Add some shrimp with the recipe. Cook it spicy and Cajun. Do some goose nuggets. Goose is no different than any other entrée, but remember – it's not a steak."

White-fronts – I've heard nothing but good things about speckle-bellies on the table. Many I've had tell me that they'd rather eat specks than any other type of waterfowl. In fact, ask a man from Louisiana or Arkansas or Texas what's the best eating kind of goose, and I can almost guarantee you that there will be absolutely NO hesitation before he shoots back – speckle-bellies.

"It's my favorite bird," says Bill Cooksey, head public relations guru for Avery Outdoors. "I've never understood why, especially since a lot of the specks that we shoot are running with snows. But young or old, it's doesn't seem to matter. They're just great."

And now how's this for a culinary testimonial? Cooksey finishes his commentary with this quote – "I can't say why, but God they're good. I'd rather eat them than teal. And I love teal." Better than teal? Now that's saying something.

Snows and blues – During the fall, Tony Toye runs his Big River Guide Service on the Mississippi River not far from his home in Boscobel, Wisconsin. Canvasbacks, when they're in season, are his specialty. Come spring, or more precisely, February, you can find Toye in the northwest corner of Missouri where he spends five to six very interesting and often frustrating weeks chasing the scores of northern-bound snows and blues that pass through the area. And he's very good at it, as you read in the chapter dealing with these oft-fickle birds; however, I digress.

In a brief electronic conversation, I asked Toye his thoughts on the reputation that white geese have been given as far as their ranking on the table is concerned. That reputation? Well, most will tell you that given the choice between snow goose and garden slugs, they'd be more than happy to deal with the slimy little critters. The slugs, that is.

"I don't think this bad reputation is justified," says Toye. "I think the reputation comes either from people who are unable to hunt them successfully. Or it may come from a time before the birds' diet switched over to grain. At one time, the birds' main diet was strictly grasses. Today, though, it's corn, peas, wheat, and other grains."

Toye, who admits that the majority of the white geese he brings home are either smoked or ground into sausage, laughed when I asked if there was such a thing as a good-eating snow goose.

"Certainly," he said, "but I would guess that the 15 to 25-year-old birds (NOTE: Toye killed a banded snow in Missouri a couple years back that was 19 years old!) are not the best of eating. A fat juvenile is an extremely good-eating bird!"

As I've said time and time again, though it's certainly not an original statement, good game on the table begins

Ask 100 guys who've eaten them, and 100 will agree – Specklebellies are the best-eating goose on the planet, bar none.

with good game care in the field. To this end, Toye offers this advice with snows - "Gut them fairly quickly, and then soak them in salt water."

So I guess I'll have to say that the jury's still out on white geese. Truth is, it's like anything else – some folks love 'em, and some folks hate 'em.

Sandhill cranes – All the while I was in Kramer, North Dakota, I heard folks talk highly about sandhill cranes. "Ribeye of the sky," they said. "Best eating game bird on the planet." So with those words ringing in my impressionable ears and, when presented with the chance, I shot my first crane. I then took my first crane back home to Iowa where Julie waited, her own head filled with my tales of "excellent table fare" and "Can't wait to try this!" To make a long story short, if I ever ate a rib eye steak that tasted like that first sandhill crane, I'd smack the cattleman who raised it clear back to Texas.

"I killed a crane in Canada," said outdoor writing colleague, Phil Bourjaily. "Now the Canadians wanted nothing to do with it. The Ducks Unlimited guys I was with took it, marinated it, and grilled it. They were big on grilling and marinating. Anyway, they did these kind of kabobs with it, and people were fighting over it. It was excellent." Bourjaily tried another, this one from North Dakota and done rare in his own oven. And that one, too, he claims was wonderful on the table.

"They're fantastic," said Derek Rambo. A one-time waterfowl guide in west-central Texas, the Dallas resident

Now the dilemma – On the wall, or on the table? Or both?

now works as a manufacturer's rep for Avery Outdoors. "I think it's because of all the grain they eat," Rambo continued. "They have some of the lightest colored meat. Not at all like liver. But then again, I have a fail-safe marinade (NOTE: Even as you read this, I'm trying to pry this recipe out of the young man) that just works wonders on anything."

So maybe – hopefully – my first crane-eating fiasco was an isolated incident, for it seems as though my taste buds are in the minority. At least in this case.

Field care

I said it in the duck book, the turkey book, the small game book, and I'm going to say it again here. Good-tasting – or foul-tasting – wild game gets its start the moment it hits the ground. It doesn't matter if we're talking Canadas or caribou, speck-bellies or Sitka blacktails. It's all the same, and it's just that simple. Sure, there are kitchen counter secrets – marinades, sauces, spices, and the like – that can accent the good, or in some cases, mask the not-so-good. Still, the care and attention you give your game, in this case geese, both in the field and immediately at home, will be reflected when it comes time for that fancy sit-down dinner with company. After all, you don't want to have the boss and his wife over for supper, only to tearfully pitch a roasted Canada that should have more accurately been stamped MICHELIN while reaching for Pizza

Hut on the speed-dial, now do you?

To tell you the truth, field care when it comes to geese is quite simple. Fact is, most hunters, myself often included, do little or nothing when it comes to physically tending to their harvested birds while still in the field, other than not piling the birds one on top of the other. Doing so creates, in essence, a feathered compost pile, and the birds at the bottom? Well, they've started cooking even before you've crawled out of the pit. Better to spread them out, out of direct sunlight if possible, so they're given a chance to cool.

Still, and despite there being few rules or guidelines regarding goose field care, there's always that old cliché – For every rule, there's an exception. Actually in my book, there are three exceptions to this "Do Nothing" rule. And these include –

Warm weather – It doesn't matter whether the high temperatures come during an early September season or a weeklong bout of Indian summer during the first days of November. Heat is heat, regardless of when, and heat is bad news when it comes to wild game.

The solution to this heat problem is simple – cooling. How? First, and as already mentioned, don't pile your birds up. Secondly, keep them in the shade. Maybe underneath a decoy or a cool back portion of the pit.

But maybe more is necessary. In some extreme cases, you might find it helpful to draw (gut) your birds right there in the field in order to facilitate this cooling process. During my early-season goose hunts, I'll always have two or three pair of disposal surgical gloves on hand, as well as a half dozen sections of mesh or cheese cloth big game bags. Oh, and a handful of zip-ties. Once a bird's killed, it's drawn – the rubber gloves keep my hands clean and my water for drinking as opposed to washing – and placed inside a "tube" of mesh bag. The bag is then sealed top and bottom with the zip-ties, and is placed in the shade. Or better yet, a cooler, if possible. Gutted, the bird cools quickly, and the mesh bag keeps flies off the carcass and dirt out of the body cavity.

White geese – Guide Tony Toye mentioned earlier that he prefers to draw his white geese as soon as humanly possible. While I can't vouch for this action myself as it pertains to snows, I certainly can't disagree with Toye's thinking here. I don't know of any game bird, the taste of which *would not* benefit from a quick and in-the-field removal of its innards. And that's for any number of reasons, one of which is -

Badly shot-up birds – It's not a pleasant thought. Shot-ravaged innards. Intestinal fluids and digestive juices slowly seeping into body cavities. An internal, all-natural marinade. Combined with 40-degree and higher temperature readings, these enzymes make quick work of…well, of taste.

A vivid example, yes, but it's presented to make a point. Gutting your birds afield, badly shot-up or no, eliminates the above-mentioned scenario altogether, and can lead to a much better tasting end product. Do we do it on a regular basis? I'm afraid not, and I'm not exactly sure why. Drawing birds afield takes but a moment, and requires neither extensive cutlery nor wild slight-of-hand; however, it *can* make a world of difference come time for the dinner bell. 'Nough said.

Separation of feathers and bird

Okay. So here's where we actually get down to the cleaning process. At this point, we're assuming that the birds have been well tended to in the field, and are now at the place – camp, lodge, home, buddy's home, what-have-you – where they're going to be made ready for the table. Or maybe they'll be headed to the freezer. Either way, there are any number of methods for separating the edible from the non-edible portions.

What you need

The equipment needed to ready your birds for the table depends almost entirely on what you plan to do with the bird in the kitchen. A whole roasted bird, perhaps a stuffed Canada intended for Christmas dinner, would be dry-plucked; therefore, all you're going to need here are strong thumbs and forefingers, a sharp knife – a heavy blade will do fine – a propane torch, and the storage materials to be discussed in a bit. Those prone to waxing will, of course, need wax and a means of melting said wax, while the skinners and the fillet fans tend toward longer, thin-bladed flexing knives. Something that allows them to work deftly around bone and underneath skin.

While we're on the subject of knives. If I'm processing a large number of geese, and particularly if I'm filleting them, I'll include a small Firestone sharpener in my cleaning kit. A half dozen passes through the ceramic wheels periodically, and I'll have a keen edge from start to finish. And finally, there's the game shears. Or the tin snips, like those that I've been using for years now.

Hanging - Before I get into the cleaning details themselves, let me take just a minute and talk about hanging. Growing up, I never had an option when it came to cleaning waterfowl. We'd pluck the feathers from around the vent, just enough to gut the bird. Then the day's bag, be they ducks, geese, or both, would be hung by the neck from the transom of my Old Man's Sears V-bottom for such a time as my Pop deemed adequate. That may be a day; it might be three. Often, the time decision was based on weather. Or more precisely, temperature. Thirty-five to 45 degrees would mean two or three days. Fifty degrees, and the day after the hunt would be designated "Plucking Day."

Now I wish I'd thought of it, but I didn't. Hanging

Goose cleaning tools are actually quite few and very elemental. A sharp knife, sharpener, tin snips, propane torch, and – if plucking – a strong thumb and forefinger.

game helps. Butchers and big game hunters alike know the benefits of leaving red meat hang at controlled temperatures. Hanging, or aging as it's often called, helps to both bring out a wild meat's natural flavor, as well as aids in tenderizing that particular cut or carcass. We did it while I was growing up, and the birds were excellent. I do it today, and the birds are wonderful. Conclusive? I don't know, but I am a big fan of the "If it ain't broke, don't fix it" credo. I *will* say this about hanging my geese, though. While admittedly an advocate, I don't subscribe to that historical rule of thumb regarding the method and length of time for hanging waterfowl; that being – "Using a stout nail, secure the goose to a wall or upright plank through the bill, and leave hang until the weight of the body causes the carcass and bill to separate."

No, sir. I'll pass on that one.

Dry-plucking - Until I moved away from home, I always dry-plucked my geese. It's the way I was taught, and there really wasn't another option. We were pluckers, my father and I. By the end of the waterfowl season, I could poke a hole through a cast-iron skillet with just my thumb; it was that strong. Today, I'm still a big fan of dry-plucking. Myself, I don't think it takes all that much time, and the end result, when stuffed and roasted a golden brown or deep-fried, is as much to the eyes as the bird itself is to the palate.

In practice, dry-plucking is easy. Using your thumb and forefinger, start with the bird on its back and begin

After removing the innards, we *always* hanged our geese for a couple days at 40 degrees or below. Some don't. I personally think it makes a difference, taste-wise.

just ahead of the vent area. The trick is to work against the grain of the feathers; that is, from tail to head. Another helpful hint – Press down against the skin firmly with your thumb while at the same time sliding your thumb forward. This downward-forward pressure helps remove the majority of the down feathers along with the outer feathers. True, some folks will use a two-step process here, removing the heavy feathers first, and then going back over the bird to pluck the down. It's really your choice.

Dry-plucking ceases when the bird is nude. Pay particular attention to the sides and around the legs and thighs. Don't worry too much about the ring of tug-resistant feathers just above the scaled portion of the leg and foot; we'll address that later. Some folks, myself included, will on occasion pluck the wings and the neck, both of which make excellent soup stock. Personally, I don't bother with the area from just ahead of the vent back to the tail tips as I'll remove this section in its entirety as the first part of the drawing process.

Which brings us to the appendages, gutting, and completion. Once you've decided on the amount of neck – Remember the soup! – you wish to keep, simply remove the head and that portion of the neck you've decided against. Here, a heavy blade with some backbone or better yet, a sharp cleaver, will make short work of this task.

Next, the wings. Regardless of whether or not you're going to use the wings, the method for removal is the same. With the now-plucked, de-headed goose on its side

– neck to the left, tail to the right for you right-handers; opposite for you lefties – grasp a wing and bend it toward the neck. This exposes what I call the "armpit" area. Now, using a heavy bladed knife, make a 45-degree cut downward perpendicular to the line of the body and at this "armpit" area. A bit more bending and a little cutting, and you'll be able to separate the wing at this major joint. Flip the bird over, and do the same on the other side. It takes a little bit of practice, but with time you'll come to know exactly where the ball-and-socket joint lies.

Now it's time for the innards. With the bird on its back, neck away, cut completely through the goose an inch or so ahead of the vent. This cut not only eliminates the vent and the next-to-nothing tail meat, but also removes the oil glands. But yes, I know what you're thinking – intestinal contents and contamination. Truth is, I've never had a problem in this regard. The cut itself results in very little spillage from the severed intestine, and the time involved between cutting and gutting is practically nil.

With the tail section removed, insert the tip of your knife, blade up, in the upper portion of the opening you've just made, and make a cut through this loose skin to either side of the point of keel. TIP – Don't go too deep. You don't want to cut through any more of the innards. TIP TWO – When you hit bone, which is the keel, stop. Now you can remove the entrails. Make sure you don't forget the lungs, which are pink spongy masses located on either side of the spine opposite the breast, and the kidneys. These dark brownish organs are found in two pockets, again on either side of the spine, just inside the opening you've made. At this point, I'm going to suggest you keep the heart, liver, and gizzard, all of which, like the neck, make excellent soup stock or gravy fixings. A simple rinsing cleans the heart and liver, while the gizzard is split lengthwise and the tough inner lining removed before giving it a thorough washing.

Minus feathers, innards, wings, tail, head, and neck, your goose is done, save for a quick singeing and final rinse. And here's why you haven't as yet removed the legs, which serve as handles during the singeing process. Singeing gets rid of all the tiny, hair-like feathers that remain after plucking, as well as any tuffs of down or pinfeathers that you might have missed. Myself, I use a propane torch to singe my birds. I've heard of folks using candles or even Zippo lighters, but a propane torch seems to work best. TIP – Don't, as I've read in the past, use a torch made of tightly-rolled newspaper or newsprint. The burning inks can impart a bad, burnt taste to the meat. When singeing, use a low flame and pay attention to what you're doing. You don't want to char the flesh just yet.

The last step is to remove the feet, including the scaled portion of the legs. Again using your heavy bladed knife, cut through the tendons at the point where the upper and lower ball joints meet. Like with the wings, a

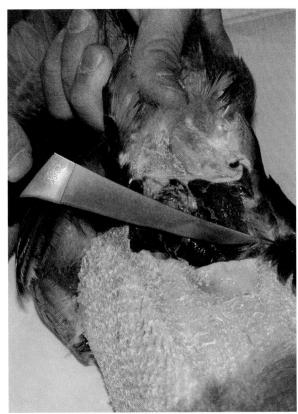

Dry-plucking is time-consuming, yes, but it makes for an awfully nice presentation on the table. Don't forget the deep fat fryer, either.

Removing the wings at the body joint takes a bit of practice, but there again, it makes for a wonderful presentation.

little bending may be necessary, as may a little practice. TIP – Using your off or non-knife wielding hand, grab hold of the foot and lift until you feel resistance or weight from the carcass. This weight stretches the tendons and opens the ball joints slightly, making it easier to locate and incise the joint. Again, it just takes practice. A rinse inside and out, and your bird's ready for oven or freezer.

Before we leave this section, let me mention scalding. Scalding is similar to dry-plucking, the difference being that the scalded birds are first dipped into very hot – not boiling – water before being plucked. The hot water, it's said, helps loosen the feathers, making them easier to remove. The key here lies in attaining the proper water temperature. Too cold, and you're doing nothing more than creating a wet, smelly mess. Too hot, and not only will you burn your hands, but you'll parboil your goose as well. Personally, I've never been really big on scalding anything except crawdads, blue crabs, and steamer clams; still, there are folks out there who would have it no other way.

Waxes and little rubber fingers – I've never actually waxed a goose. Nor have I ever witnessed the act; however, I've had folks tell me that they use this age-old method for denuding waterfowl and say that it works quite well. I'll take their word for it.

Waxing is just as it sounds. A mixture of bee's wax and paraffin, or a commercially made "Duck Wax," is melted in a large pot or kettle. The birds, with wings removed, are dipped into the wax, and the coating allowed to harden. Once it sets, the wax is then peeled or broken off, and with it comes feathers, down, pinfeathers…the whole 9 yards…leaving nothing but a naked bird ready for evisceration. The fuzzy chunks of paraffin are thrown back into the melting pot, and the process repeated. To me, it sounds like a lot of work, equipment, effort, and mess, but there are folks who swear by it. Your choice.

As for the little rubber fingers, here's the story there. Picture, if you will, a drum sander. But instead of a sanding belt, the drum is studded with 25 to 30 rubber fingers each ¾ of an inch in diameter. You flick the ON switch, and the drum begins to rotate at a high rate of speed. Next, you take a goose, hold it against the spinning fingers, and VOILA! No more feathers. No more skin on your knuckles, but no more feathers either. Technically, they're called Pickers, and essentially they serve the same purpose as do your thumbs and forefingers…only faster, and with less arthritic pain. Commercial outfits like the Duck Naked – I love it! – Duck Picker operate on a ⅓-horsepower motor and are designed to sit atop a 55-gallon drum, which is meant to catch and contain at least some of the feathers. Smaller self-driven models can be mounted to a workbench, while still others are meant to be chucked into a ⅜-inch electric drill. All in all, the pickers with their little rubber fingers work well; I've watched them get a goose nude in what seemed like seconds. Still, unless you're cleaning a hell of a lot of geese, you might want to think about the fact that you already have the world's best pluck-

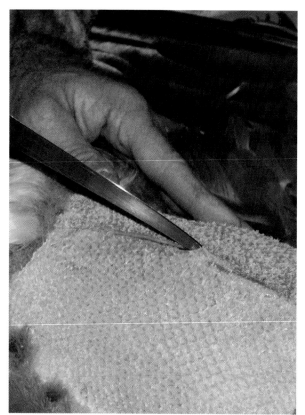

Quick and easy, skinning is preferred by many; however, it does eliminate that most excellent moisture-retention device during the cooking process – the skin.

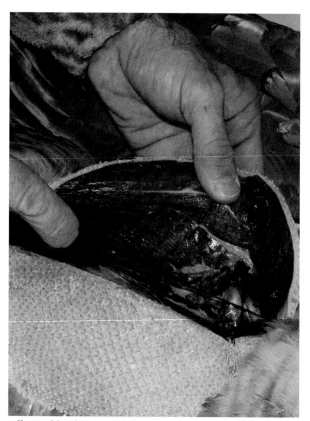

Filleting, like skinning, is a fast and simply method of separating edible from non-edible. When filleting, I always keep the legs and thighs for soup meat.

ers right there at the end of your wrists.

Skinning – Here's my take on skinning geese. One, the skin lends quite a bit of flavor to the meat during the cooking process. Two, unlike some skins – chicken comes to mind – eating goose skin isn't all that bad for you, and actually can be nutritious. Finally, and perhaps most significantly, skinning your geese totally eliminates the planet's finest roasting bag. The secret to moist, tender waterfowl. That's right, the skin.

All right. That said, let's take a quick look at skinning. To be honest, I know few waterfowlers who skin their geese. Maybe their upland birds, fowl such as pheasants and grouse and chukars, but not geese. A handful of the reasons behind this, I'm sure, are those listed above. Another might be the plain and simple fact that skinning most waterfowl is akin to skinning a steel-belted radial; that is, it's a tough way to go. Now, I won't say that a Canada's skin sticks like that of a bluebill, redhead, or ringneck, but it's pretty sticky nonetheless. My point? If you're going to skin it, you may as well breast it; however, I digress.

Skinning. Using a sharp, thin-bladed knife, cut through the skin on one side or the other of the breast bone (keel). From this point, it's actually a simple matter, working primarily with your fingers only, to peel and pull the skin away from the breast. A little trimming will be necessary, particularly around the more bony areas like the upper sides and the back. Remove any fat that clings

to the meat, paying attention to the breast and legs, and the task is complete.

Filleting - Myself, I'm torn here. Yes, filleting is a quick, easy, and efficient method of cleaning geese, especially when there are a large number to be processed. But, yes, filleting also wastes the meat on the back (soup stock), the legs (soup), and thighs (soup or stir-fry). And, too, unless they retain the skin, those who would fillet must compensate for the moisture loss the skin prevents during the cooking process. Still, filleting has grown tremendously in popularity among the nation's goose hunters in recent years. And I must count myself among this crowd as today, I fillet perhaps 75 percent of the geese that we kill. I do save all our legs and thighs, thus minimizing to some extent our waste, but...

When I talk filleting, also known as breasting the birds out, I'm speaking of two variations – bone-in, and bone-out. Let's start with bone-out. This is probably the most familiar form of filleting, with the breast halves (the fillets) removed entirely. The process is quick, and leaves you with two very nice-sized boneless breasts. These can then be grilled whole, steaked, cubed, chunked, stir-fried, or any of a thousand different things.

The process of bone-out filleting is quite simple, and involves no plucking whatsoever. With my knife blade up – I use a seven to nine-inch flexible fillet knife for this – I insert the tip underneath the skin at the bottom of the breast; that is, just ahead of the vent. I then run the blade forward along the breast bone, or keel, to the point where the V-shaped collarbone and keel intersect. Laying the blade aside and using my fingers, I slowly pull the skin away from each breast half. TIP – Be sure to peel the skin well past the ribs. This ensures it won't be in the way during the actual filleting step.

With the breast halves thus exposed, I make two cuts – one on the left side of the left "arm" of the V (collarbone) and down to the point of the breast above the vent, and the second on the right side. Make certain to maintain blade-to-bone down along the "arm," as well as the breast bone. Once these cuts have been made, it's a simple matter to lift the fillet away from the breast plate – the bone underneath – and slice the meat away. To tell you the truth, it's not much different than filleting over a walleye's ribs. A little knife work down against the bone, and it's done.

I like bone-in filleting myself. Not only is it quicker, but because the bone remains a part of the whole, it's mass helps in retaining moisture during cooking. When doing a bone-in fillet, I swap my thin blade for a heavier bladed knife. And you'll see why in a minute.

Starting again with the breast exposed, I make my initial cut downward and perpendicular to the keel at the point where the breast ends ahead of the vent. Turning my knife blade toward the bird's head, I cut through the ribs on either side to the wing joints, or "armpit." Now the entire breast can be pulled upward; however, it's still connected at the wing joints and at the collarbone. A little surgery with the tip of my knife separates the wing joint tendons, and a clip-clip with my tin snips handles the clavicle on either side. TIP – Take care whenever using shears or snips to cut bone as the cutting action can and often does produce sharp shards.

An equally quick variation on the skinless bone-in method involves plucking just the breast and side feathers, and then proceeding as before. With the breast detached, a propane torch takes care of any pinfeathers or down. It's a small step, I realize, but it does save the skin. And together with the bone, the combination can truly make a difference in the moisture content of the final product.

Storage – How you store your processed geese depends on one thing – the length of time between cleaning and eating. Let's assume that your birds are cleaned to your liking and rinsed well. Now what?

Well, if you're going to make a meal of him within the next 24 to 48 hours, I'd suggest placing the fillets, the bone-in breast, or the whole bird into either a heavy-duty Zip-lock bag or plastic wrap-covered dish, and putting the whole thing in the refrigerator. Any longer than 48 hours, and you need to be thinking about some type of long-term storage.

Okay, long-term storage. If you plan on digging into your birds within the next month, you'll be all right storing them in quality – key word: quality – freezer bags.

Mummify the breasts or fillets in plastic wrap, and slip them inside the bag, making sure to squeeze as much of the air out as possible before sealing. TIP – Zip all but an inch or so of your Zip-loc bags closed, and immerse everything but the unzipped corner into a five-gallon bucket filled with water. The water pressure forces most of the air out of the bag, giving you a near vacuum seal. But be quick on that zipper.

If your bird's destined to live in the deep-freeze for more than a month, I'd strongly suggest a vacuum sealer. Yes, they can be a little bit spendy, ranging anywhere from $150 to $300, but hey, aren't you shooting ammunition that costs $1.50 a round? And what's less expensive? A one-time purchase of a name-brand vacuum packer, or throwing most of last year's crop of waterfowl out in the trash because it's been freezer-burnt beyond recognition? That said, let me finish by saying that today's vacuum packers are user-friendly, and, if it's cost that concerns you, can be used for a lot more than simply sucking the wind out of bags of deceased geese. The bottom line? You can't go wrong with a vacuum packer.

Finally, whole birds. Whole birds pose a little more of a logistical problem when it comes to wrapping and storage; however, it's not an impossible problem. You can try huge Zip-lock style bags, the kind that Babe Winkelman talks about on his "Outdoor Secrets" show. And it's not a bad idea, the Zip-lock bags. Lacking those, however, I've trussed more than one dressed Canada tightly in plastic wrap, followed by several layers of newspaper, and finally, an outer covering of butcher or freezer paper – all sealed and held together with wide masking tape. Time limit? Three to six months, maximum. Any more, and you'll be flirting with Mister Freezer Burn.

In the kitchen

If geese were beer, I'm sure that there'd be folks who would describe them as being full-bodied. A bold, definitive flavor, they might add. And I can't disagree there. Migratory waterfowl do indeed have a flavor all their own. Some love it, and some hate it. There's really, as my father used to say, no in-between. It doesn't taste like chicken, for the benefit of those who were about to ask. And it really doesn't taste like liver, though if I were pressed to make a comparison - with qualifiers – between wild goose and anything that the general public might be more familiar with, it would probably have to be liver. This isn't a comparison based on similar tastes, mind you, as I'd as soon eat glue than liver, but rather on looks and texture. And some would even say cooking techniques.

There's a difference, you see, between the goose that Emeril Lagusse puts on his countertop, and the ones that those of you who are reading these words will have. And that major difference? As far as birds go, Emeril's goose

Vacuum packing is THE way to go for storing your birds; that is, unless you're going to prepare them within two to three weeks. Any longer, use the sucker.

lived what I'll call a life of leisure. Relatively speaking, of course. Mr. Lagusse's bird never migrated, so he never developed those incredibly strong – translation: potentially tough – pectoral muscles that your wild bird did. And I'm willing to bet that Emeril's goose never picked peas in an Alberta field or grubbed for grasses along the edge of a Louisiana salt marsh. Nope, that bird was catered to, again relatively speaking, courtesy of a five-pound coffee can filled with cracked corn. Your bird? He worked for a living, plain and simple.

So what's this all have to do with wild geese, how they taste, and what you do with them in the kitchen? You treat wild geese differently, that's all. You keep them moist. You cook them rare. Medium rare at the very most. You use a little spice here and little spice there. Maybe a little bacon. Perhaps a roasting bag. You treat 'em with love and care. After all, it's like Tommy Stutzman said – "You can't just slap 'em on the grill, smother 'em in sauce, and expect 'em to taste like that last sirloin you had." No, sir. Wild geese need a little bit more than that, but believe you me, it's worth it. Every minute.

As Don Johnson said in his wonderful book, *Grouse & Woodcock: A Gunner's Guide*, "Since this is not a cookbook, I'm going to refrain from discussing any preparations at great length," I too will not go into any great detail regarding the 101 different goose recipes already tried and tested. Nor will I expound upon the 1,001 taste sensations just waiting in the proverbial wings – no pun intended –

to be discovered; however, and you knew that was coming, I do feel it necessary to mention just a handful of some of the finer recipes I've come across over the past two decades since that evening behind my grandfather's farm, the night I became a goose hunter.

Roast goose – About twice a year, I'll get a hankering for a whole roast wild Canada goose. Nothing elaborate, just a young bird roasted golden brown. Just enough for myself and Julie, along with a couple friends. On such occasions, I'll treat the guest of honor – a nice Canada – in just such a manner.

Rinse and dry a 6- to 7-pound Canada inside and out. Salt and pepper liberally, again inside and out, followed by a light misting – Like that? – with spray margarine or butter. Fill the cavity with chunked apples, peeled oranges, and sweet onions, and truss the opening closed with toothpicks. Or better yet, sew it shut with butcher's twine.

Now place the bird, breast down, in a good, solid roasting pan. Drizzle fresh orange juice, the kind with lots of pulp, over the top. Fresh oranges, rolled and squeezed, can also be used; however, if you do that, make sure you drop the de-juiced sections into the bottom of the roaster. Flavor, don't you know. With doubled heavy-duty aluminum foil, cover the bird securely. Again, securely.

Crank the oven up to 500 degrees and put the bird in. At the end of an hour, take the bird out, uncover it, and flip it breast-up. TIP – An extra set of hands really helps at this point in the game. Re-cover securely, turn the over down to 350 degrees, and roast for another hour or so. Play with the time, and remember you want the juice to run slightly pink when the breast is pricked with a fork. Remove the cover and run the bird another 15 minutes or so. Just enough to get that golden brown glow. Serve with rice, potatoes, asparagus, green salad…damn near anything.

Good? Let me put it this way. My Ma, who's not a big fan of waterfowl, absolutely loved wild goose done this way. 'Nough for me.

Goose jerky – I'm not *even* going to try to say that this jerky recipe is THE one and only jerky recipe to use. Everyone and his or her brother – or sister – has a jerky recipe, and some of them are awful good. Julie and I sort of stumbled onto this one by accident, and truth be known, it changes just slightly each time we put it together. A little more of this, a little less of that. 'Course if there's an open beer on the counter at the time…well, let's just say that in my kitchen, Pabst Blue Ribbon goes into a lot of different things. Anyway –

On your goose breast fillets, make sure you slice them across the grain. If you don't, your jerky's going to be awful tough and chewy. Too, it helps if your goose is semi-frozen when you're working with it. Makes it easier to cut. Oh, and ¼-inch slices should do just fine.

In a glass or crockery bowl – no metal – combine and

Each year, I make a big batch of goose jerky using both my smoker and the household oven. Funny, it never seems to last long.

thoroughly mix the following. Remember, your ingredients, amounts, and beer of choice may vary.

- 1 package fajita seasoning
- 1 teaspoon Johnny's salt
- ¾ teaspoon liquid smoke
- 1¼ teaspoon black pepper
- ¾ teaspoon minced garlic or garlic powder
- ½ teaspoon onion powder
- 1¼ teaspoon salt
- 7 dashes, aka A Little Bit, Worcestershire sauce
- 4 drops – I use *a lot* more – Tabasco sauce or other hot sauce
- ½ can Pabst Blue Ribbon beer
- enough water to get everything nice and dissolved

Combine the goose breast slices and the marinade in a large non-metal bowl, cover with plastic wrap, and put in the 'fridge. Typically, I let my jerky brine for a minimum of 24 hours, and often I'll let it sit 48 hours.

Once the brining is complete, drain the liquid. Rinse and pat dry the slices thoroughly. Now, you can use your favorite smoker for the drying process; however, I'm still a huge fan of the oven. All you do is line the bottom rack with aluminum foil, in essence making it an improvised drip pan, and place it as low as it will go. Turn the heat on LOW – our lowest setting is 170 degrees, which seems to be about perfect. Slide a round toothpick through one end of each slice, and hang it between the grills in the upper rack, itself set as high as it will go. Continue until the rack

is complete. Prop the door open so the moisture you're driving out of the meat can escape, and – now the painful part – wait. Drying time is guesswork, so you'll just have to periodically sample some slices to determine their progress. Tough job, but someone has to do it. Store your jerky, if there's any left, in open Zip-lock bags.

Goose stir-fry – A simple one, and not a bad recipe for young snow geese.

- 1 to 2 goose breast fillets sliced across the grain into finger-sized pieces
- 1 to 1½ cups – sliced carrots, onions, broccoli, celery, cauliflower, or –
- 1 bag of ready-to-go Stir-Fry vegetables (I usually take this route)
- 1 can sliced water chestnuts

For this next step, I have no measurements as I always just eye-ball the concoction until it looks about right. That, and stick my finger in it from time to time for a taste test. I'd suggest you doing the same, just wash your hands first.

In a mixing bowl, combine various amounts of the following –

- Soy sauce – Quite a bit of this
- Hot sesame oil
- Tabasco
- Salt and pepper (freshly ground black works best)
- Sugar
- Watkins garlic oil or garlic powder

- Onion powder
- Italian dressing
- 1 packet of either taco or fajita seasoning
- water

To finish, quick-fry the goose breast slices in a heavy skillet to which you've added a bit of olive oil. Drain and set aside. Add a bit more oil and quick-fry your vegetables until they're hot through, but still crispy. Toss the meat back in with the vegetables, dump your liquid on top, and simmer for five to 10 minutes. Not too long as you don't want the veggies to get soggy. Serve over Ramen noodles or rice.

Corned goose – This one comes from Kevin Michalowski – editor, friend, and die-hard waterfowler – who assures me that it "tastes a lot like corned beef...only better." I myself haven't tried it, and I have to admit that I was a bit leery. After all, this is the same guy who had damn near an entire deer made into ring bologna – 76 pounds worth. Would you trust this guy?

- Skinned breast fillets from one goose
- 4 cups water
- ¾ cup Tender Quick pickling salt
- 1 tablespoon pickling spices
- ½ teaspoon caraway seed
- 1 onion, sliced

Place the goose in a non-metal container and arrange the onion slices over the top. Sprinkle on the spices and cover with a mixture of salt and water. Make sure the meat is completely covered. Let soak for 24 hours, turn the fillets, and soak for an additional 24 hours. Drain and rinse thoroughly. The fillets can be roasted at 350 degrees until tender. Time? I'm going to guess right around 1½ hours. Remember – moist heat.

Braised Canada goose with orange sauce – Kris Winkelman of Babe Winkelman Productions, as talented an outdoor chef as her husband is an angler, was oh-so-kind enough to not only let me bother her one afternoon with cooking questions, but gave me her blessing to use the following recipe here.

"We go out to eat at so many different restaurants, and I'm always looking to try something different," Kris told me. "Something other than the steak and the chicken. That, and I really like sauces. I like to pick them apart and see what they're made of. And this," she laughed, "was as close as I could come without actually asking for the recipe." And with that, Kris' Braised Goose with orange sauce.

Wash a whole dressed Canada – 7 pounds or so – inside and out, and stuff with –

- ½ onion
- 3 celery stalks, chopped
- 3 carrot sticks, chopped

Place the bird in a roasting pan and add –
- 2 cups homemade goose stock or chicken stock
- 1 cup red wine

The bird, covered, goes into a 250-degree oven for 2 hours, or until when pricked with a fork, the juices run clear. Remove the cover for the final 15 minutes or until the skin is brown and crispy. De-bone the bird, keeping the breast and leg/thigh in one large piece. Set aside, covered.

Drain the fat from the roasting pan, and strain carefully through cheesecloth. In a saucepan, combine the fat with –

- ¾ cup fresh orange juice
- ¼ teaspoon dry mustard
- ½ cup dry red wine
- salt and pepper to taste

- and warm over medium-high heat. To thicken the sauce, add a roux or cornstarch dissolved in white wine or cold water. Play with the seasonings until you have the flavor you wish, and when it's there, add the goose pieces just long enough to warm them through. Serve with wild rice or mashed potatoes.

Here's something Kris mentioned while we were talking about geese and their tendency to be tough.

"There's no better way," she said, "to get rid of the toughness of geese, or any waterfowl for that matter, than with a pressure cooker. A lot of people are so alarmed about pressure cookers. That they're going to blow up or whatever. That just doesn't happen anymore, not with the modern safety valves and features the cookers have. Even the old cookers can be fitted with modern safety features."

"I add my seasonings before putting the goose into the cooker," she continued, "so everything can cook together. A little chicken broth and a little water. It just works very well."

Okay, so perhaps I wasn't a brief as I might have been here. My sincere apologies to Mister Don Johnson; however, I'd like to end on this note.

If you're ever in Kramer, North Dakota, during the last couple weeks of October, do me a favor and stop into the old school building where Dean Kersten of Central Flyway Outfitters has set up shop. Ask – beg if you have to – if Dean would be nice enough to let you sample the goose that the local ladies have prepared for his hunters. Done up in big white roaster ovens, the meal's served in the school's former gymnasium. Yep, right here on the stage overlooking the spar-varnished basketball court, the same stage where the flute-a-phone concerts were held, and where the fourth-graders presented their version of "A Christmas Story" each year for Lord only knows how many.

And when you're finished, and you're in fear of wearing a hole in the front of your shirt from rubbing your belly, think about this – that's goose gravy drying on your chin. Wild goose. And ponder the question: "I wonder what the non-hunters are eating tonight?"

Manufacturers, agencies, and outfitters

Drake Waterfowl
910 E. Goodman Rd.
Suite F
Southaven, MS 38671
662-349-9398
www.drakewaterfowl.com

Ballistic Specialties
PO Box 2401
Batesville, AR 72503
800-276-2550
www.angleport.com

Coyote Company Leather
3706 Yaupon Dr.
Grand Prairie, TX 75052
www.coyotecoleather.com

Central Flyway Game Calls
608 Main St.
Beaver Crossing, NE 68313
402-532-2150
www.callemclose.com

Haydel's Game Calls
5018 Hazel Jones Rd.
Bossier City, LA 71111
318-746-3586
www.haydels.com

Hard Core Decoys
214 E. 34th St.
Garden City, ID 83714
www.hardcoredecoys.com

Final Approach Blinds
Kolpin Outdoors
205 N. Depot St.
Fox Lake, WI 53933
877-956-5746
www.finalapproach blinds.com

O.F. Mossberg & Sons
7 Grasso Ave.
North Haven, CT 06473
www.mossberg.com

Randy Bartz & Flagman Products
Box 301
Oronoco, MN 55960
800-575-4782
www.flagmanproducts.com

Vito A. Angelone
Widgeon Bay Watermen
1200 N. Timber Ridge Rd.
Cross Junction, VA 22625
www.widgeonbaywatermen.com

Arborwear
PO Box 341
Chagrin Falls, OH 44022
1-888-578-TREE
www.arborwear.com

Flambeau Products
PO Box 97
Middlefield, OH 44062
www.flamprod.com

Remington Arms Company
870 Remington Dr.
Madison, NC 27025
www.remington.com

Winchester
427 N. Shamrock St.
East Alton, IL 49685
www.winchester.com

Browning
One Browning Place
Morgan, UT 84050
www.browning.com

Big River Game Calls
4500 Doniphan Dr.
Neosho, MO 64850
www.outland-sports.com

Mossy Oak Clothing
PO Box 757
West Point, MS 39773
www.mossyoak.com

Realtree
PO Box 9638
Columbus, GA 31908
www.realtree.com

Foiles Migrators, Inc.
800 W. Quincy St.
Pleasant Hill, IL 62366
217-734-1434
www.foilesstraitmeat.com

Federal Cartridge Co.
900 Ehlen Dr.
Anoka, MN 55303
www.federalcartridge.com

DeLorme Mapping
Two Delorme Dr.
Yarmouth, ME 04096
www.delorme.com

Rocky Shoes & Boots
39 Canal St.
Nelsonville, OH 45764
www.rockyboots.com

C.C. Filson
PO Box 34020
Seattle, WA 98124
www.filson.com

Columbia Sportswear
6600 N. Baltimore
Portland, OR 97283
www.columbia.com

Bushnell Sports Optics
9200 Cody
Overland Park, KS 66214
www.bushnell.com

Nikon Sport Optics
1300 Walt Whitman Rd.
Melville, NY 11747
www.nikonusa.com

Bass Pro Shops
2500 E. Kearney
Springfield, MO 65898
www.basspro.com

Cabela's
One Cabela's Drive
Sidney, NE 69160
www.cabelas.com

Birchwood Casey
7900 Fuller Rd.
Eden Prairie, MN 55344
www.birchwoodcasy.com

Bug-Out Outdoorwear
22111 230th Ave.
Centerville, IA 52544
www.bug-out-outdoor wear.com

Ralston Purina
Checkerboard Square
St. Louis, MO 63164
1-800-7-PURINA

Goose Buster Products
Jeremy Mellick
PO Box 7461
Covington, WA 98042
www.goosebusterboys.com

Expedite Intl., Inc.
906 Dominion Dr.
Hudson, WI 54016
www.trumotion.com

Avery Outdoors
PO Box 820176
Memphis, TN 38112
901-324-1500
www.averyoutdoors.com

Manufacturers, agencies, and outfitters (continued)

Quaker Boy Game Calls
5455 Webster Rd.
Orchard Park, NY 14127
www.quakerboygame
calls.com

Gerber Legendary Blades
14200 SW 72nd Ave.
Portland, OR 97223
www.gerberblades.com

**Knight & Hale Game
Calls**
Drawer 670
Cadiz, KY 42211
www.knight-hale.com

Tender Corporation
PO Box 290
Littleton Industrial Park
Littleton, NH 03561
www.tendercorp.com

Hunter's Specialties
6000 Huntington Ct. NE
Cedar Rapids, IA 52402
www.hunterspec.com

MOJO Decoys
PO Box 1640
Bastrop, LA 71221
www.MojoMallard.com

Kent Cartridge Inc.
PO Box 849
Kearneysville, WV 25430
www.kentgamebore.com

Bill Saunders' Calls
1008 W. 37th Place
Kennewick, WA 99337
509-582-0190
www.guideseriescalls.com

Aero Outdoors
316 East "B" Circle
Pasco, WA 99301
509-545-8000
www.aerooutdoors.com

**Tim Grounds
Championship Calls**
1414 Barham St.
Johnston City, IL 62951
618-983-5649
www.timgrounds.com

Blackwater Decoy Co.
PO Box 907
Perrysburg, OH 43552
www.duckdecoys.com

George Lynch
Lynch Mob Calls
13110 W. US 223
Manitou Beach, MI 49253
517-467-2007

Federal, regional, state, and local agencies

**North Dakota Game &
Fish Department**
100 N. Bismarck
Expressway
Bismarck, ND 58501

**Long Beach Visitor's
Bureau**
PO Box 562
Long Beach, WA 98631
www.funbeach.com

**Trumbull County
Convention & Visitor's
Bureau**
650 Youngstown-Warren
Rd.
Niles, OH 44446
800-672-9555
www.trumbullcountycvb.org

**South Dakota
Department of Tourism**
711 E. Wells Ave.
Pierre, SD 57501
800-S-DAKOTA
www.travelsd.com

**Kansas Department of
Wildlife and Parks**
512 SE 25th Ave.
Pratt, KS 67124
620-672-5911
www.kdwp.state.ks.us

**Kansas Travel &
Tourism**
Kansas Department of
Commerce & Housing
800-2-KANSAS
www.travelks.org

**Nebraska Division of
Travel & Tourism**
PO Box 98907
Lincoln, NE 68509
877-NEBRASKA
www.visitnebraska.org

**Williamson (IL) County
Tourism Bureau**
PO Box 1088
Marion, IL 62959
1-800-GEESE99

Outfitters

Sandhills Adventures
Delten & Tracy Rhoades
PO Box 152
Brewster, NE 68821
www.sandhills-advetures.com

Mallardith NW Adventures
Bruce Meredith
81025 E. Wpainitia Rd.
Maupin, OR 97037
541-980-1922
www.mallardith.com

Matt Porter
Porter's Hunt Club
703 Porten Rd.
McHenry, IL 60050
847-639-8590
www.portersoutdoors.com

Tony Toye
Big River Guide Service
43605 CTH E
Boscobel, WI 53805
email:toyedecoys@tds.net

Ben Holten
North Flight Waterfowl
PO Box 463
Richland, WA 99352
509-521-8387
www.northflightwaterfowl.com

Tim Grounds
Tim Grounds Legendary Hunts
1414 Barham St.
Johnston City, IL 62951
618-983-5649
www.timgrounds.com

Tom & Judy Usunier
Big Grass Outfitters
Box 188
Plumas, Manitoba,
Canada R0J 1P0
www.biggrassoutfitters.com

Leo Lambert
Wild Wings Guides & Outfitters
35 Benbow Rd.
Winnipeg, Manitoba,
Canada R2R 1J5
www.wildwingsguide.homestead.com

Dean Kersten
Central Flyway Outfitters
576 County Road 20 NE
Kramer, ND 58748
701-228-3455

Paul Sullivan
Burbank Goose Club
370 McNary Ridge Rd.
Burbank, WA 99323
509-545-8000
www.burbankgoose.com

Allen-Curtis Waterfowl
Adventures
1220 Sikes Ave.
Sikeston, MO 63801
573-380-0032
www.wildfowladventures.com

Tommy Stutzman
Central Flyway Game Calls
608 Main St.
Beaver Crossing, NE
68313
402-532-2150
www.callemclose.com

Kelley Powers
Final Flight Outfitters
6002 Martin Highway
Union City, TN 38261
1-866-FLIGHT9
www.finalflight.net

Glenn Lancaster
Glenn's Goose Club
9336 Old Route 13
Marion, IL 62959
270-826-4364 (in-season)

Aaron Volkmar
Folded Wings, Inc.
PO Box 41155
Des Moines, IA 50311
515-490-5690

Conservation organizations and other folks

Ducks Unlimited
One Waterfowl Way
Memphis, TN 38120
901-758-3825
www.ducks.org

Delta Waterfowl
1305 E. Central Ave.
Bismarck, ND 58502
701-222-8857
www.deltawaterfowl.org

National Mossberg Collectors Association
Vic and Cheryl Havlin
PO Box 487
Festus, MO 63028
636-937-6401
www.mossbergcollectors.org

Internet Resources

The Duck Hunter's Refuge – *www.duckhunter.net*

Flocknocker – *www.flocknocker.com*

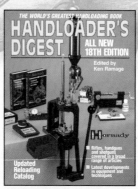

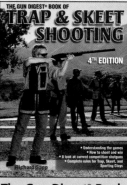